I0418668

# LOS ANGELES
# WITH

# K I D S

## 250+ ideas for ways to have fun, explore SoCal, and never have a boring weekend again

MOMSLA

Los Angeles with Kids

MomsLA.com

Copyright 2022

ISBN: 979-8-9861597-0-6

Photography and copywriting by MomsLA, LLC

Design and illustration by Caroline De Vita

All rights reserved. No part of this publication may be reproduced, stored in a retrieval system, or transmitted in any form or by any means (including electronic, mechanical, photocopying recording, or otherwise) without prior written permission.

For information about custom editions, special sales, and premium and corporate purchases, please contact MomsLA Info@MomsLA.com.

MomsLA, LLC has made every effort to ensure the accuracy of all information contained in this guide. However, all details are subject to change.

Printed in the United States of America

*"Life doesn't come with a manual,*
*it comes with a parent."*
- Unknown

*"LA didn't come with a manual - until now.*
*You're welcome."*
- MomsLA

This book is dedicated to families in Los Angeles
who want to get out there and have fun!

# ·: Table of Contents ·:

- Griffith Park Pony Rides
- Griffith Observatory
- Guinness World Record Museum
- Hollywood Bowl
- Hollywood Forever Cemetery
- Hollywood Museum
- Hollywood Sign
- Hollywood Walk of Fame
- Hollywood Wax Museum
- Los Angeles Zoo
- Ripley's Believe It or Not!
- Travel Town Museum

- Adamson House
- Annenberg Community Beach House
- Aquarium of the Pacific
- Baldwin Hills Scenic Overlook
- Battleship IOWA in San Pedro
- Beverly Hills Rodeo Drive
- Cabrillo Marine Aquarium
- Catalina Island
- Douglas Park Santa Monica
- Korean Friendship Bell
- Malibu Beaches
- Malibu Creek State Park
- Mother's Beach Marina del Rey

- Palisades Park + Camera Obscura
- Santa Monica Pier
- STAR Eco Station
- Temescal Gateway Canyon Hike
- Theatricum Botanicum
- Tongva Park Santa Monica
- Topanga Canyon horseback riding
- UCLA campus
- Venice Beach and Boardwalk, Venice Canals, and Venice Skate Park
- Will Rogers State Park

- Castle Park
- Descanso Gardens
- Frank G. Bonelli Park
- Fiesta Village Family Fun Park
- Huntington Library and Gardens
- Jet Propulsion Lab (JPL)
- Logan's Candies
- Los Angeles County Arboretum
- Los Angeles River Center and Bike Path
- March Field Air Museum
- Mariachi Plaza
- Moonlight Rollerway
- Mission Inn and Museum
- Palm Springs

- Discovery Cube LA and OC
- GRAMMY Museum
- Getty Center Museum and Getty Villa
- Heritage Square Museum
- Huntington Library, Art Museum and Botanical Gardens
- Japanese American National Museum
- Kidseum at the Bowers Museum
- Kidspace Children's Museum
- La Brea Tar Pits
- La Plaza de Cultura y Artes
- Los Angeles County Museum of Art (LACMA)
- Los Angeles Fire Department Museum
- Los Angeles Zoo
- Lucas Museum of Narrative Art
- March Field Air Museum
- Museum of Flying Santa Monica
- Museum of Latin American Art
- Natural History Museum
- Petersen Automotive Museum
- Pretend City Children's Museum
- Ronald Reagan Presidential Library and Museum
- Skirball Cultural Center
- Travel Town Museum
- USC Pacific Asia Museum
- Zimmerman Automobile Driving Museum

# Introduction

We love LA! And we think it's a great place to raise a family: the weather is pretty much always perfect, and there's almost always something super fun to do with your kids.

So we want to help you take advantage of that, and to help you get out there and enjoy everything LA has to offer!

On any given day, there are hundreds of things you could be doing with your kids in Southern California. How are you supposed to choose from a seemingly infinite list of options? How do you know which ones your kids will enjoy, much less the ones you'll want to do, too?

Let us help.

MomsLA.com was created by a team of Moms out of a desire to help other Moms (and Dads, too) get the information they need to make great choices. We think our website is the best resource for helping parents find things to do with Kids. Not only will you find super awesome lists for weekend fun (updated every week), you'll also find our great Summer Camp Guide,

Education Guide, Birthday Guide, Travel Guide - yes, we've got a guide for pretty much everything you'll need!

We created this book so you could have a handy way to carry it all around with you, in book form. It's a real printed book, so you'll get to turn the pages, bookmark your favorite section, spill coffee on it and everything. *Try doing that with a website!*

We know you're busy raising your family and living your LA Life, so relax and let us do the research work for you.

In this book, you'll find things to do divided into regions, annual events listed by season, and a list of all the Kid-friendly museums and cultural institutions we think are great. Plus we've added special sections for Things to do with Toddlers as well as Teens: Toddlers because that's the age that demands the most attention from us as parents, and Teens because that's the age when they want the least to do with us - and we just want to find *some* common ground.

A word about Parks and Beaches:

You can never go wrong taking your kids to a park or the beach.

We're blessed to be able to play at over 650 City, County, and State parks that cover more than 85,000 acres, and we can splash and get sandy along the coast on over 150 miles of beaches.

From the Mountains to the Sea, from the Deserts to the Valleys, you and your kids can have fun outdoors in every corner of Southern California - year round. Amazing, right?!

Because of that embarrassment of riches, we're not including every single park or beach in this book, because they would have run out of ink halfway through printing. But we hope you'll try them all out and find your favorites. Take it from us - you'll find amazing places!

You can find more information and all the parks and beaches in Southern California by checking out the following government agencies:

LA City Recreation and Parks Department
https://www.laparks.org/

LA County Department of Parks and Recreation
https://parks.lacounty.gov/

LA County Beaches and Harbors
https://beaches.lacounty.gov/

California State Parks
https://www.parks.ca.gov/

*Disclaimer:*

When we wrote this book, we made every effort to confirm that everything - all the details and facts about every place and event we included - was correct at the time of publication. But the world is a fluid place, and things change all the time. A favorite business may move or close, or one of the Museums might change their hours or admission prices.

Therefore, we encourage you to check with each venue before going; use their website or social media channels for up-to-the-minute info.

And consult MomsLA.com, where we can make updates more frequently.

## ABOUT MOMSLA

**"Making a Big City feel like a Hometown."**

Since 2010, MomsLA has been a trusted source for LA Moms - and Dads! We help you find the best Things to Do with Kids, you've got to check it out! MomsLA publishes the Top LA Summer Camp Guide every year, an Education Guide to LA County Schools, Online and Enrichment Programming, lists of fun Things to Do in over 65 Neighborhoods around SoCal, Birthday Party Ideas, Family Travel Ideas, Family Health and Wellness, and so much more.

Check out MomsLA.com and sign up to get our Weekly Email Newsletter!

## OUR TEAM

MomsLA is a Mom-owned business and is 100% a Team Effort. We're Moms raising families here in SoCal, so you can take our word for it: You'll find all the best things to do with kids based on our personal experiences.

Sarah Auerswald is the co-founder, and she edits and publishes MomsLA.com and is responsible for putting together this book. She and Tracy Fredkin (of @SoCalMoms on Instagram) make up the management team of MomsLA. Wendy Kennar (of WendyKennar.com) has been contributing her terrific writing to the site on a weekly basis for over 8 years!

This book is a compilation of content by all the contributors to MomsLA, including Wendy Kennar, Yvonne Condes (of YvonneInLA.com - and one of the co-Founders of MomsLA), Esther Blair (of MarkelAndMe.com), and Julia Frey (of JuliasMexicoCity.com). And we couldn't keep the proverbial website lights on without Kim Fox (of WhiteFoxCreative.com). This awesome book design and original illustrations are done by Caroline De Vita (of CarolineDeVita.com).

# DOWNTOWN L.A.

101

110

OLVERA STREET

GRAND PARK FOUNTAIN

WALT DISNEY CONCERT HALL

UNION STATION

CHINESE AMERICAN MUSEUM

LA CENTRAL LIBRARY

ANGELS FLIGHT

101

LITTLE TOKYO

GRAND CENTRAL MARKET

CITY HALL

BRADBURY BUILDING

LA LIVE

THE LAST BOOKSTORE

110

ARTS DISTRICT

101

10

FASHION DISTRICT

NATURAL HISTORY MUSEUM

110

CALIFORNIA SCIENCE CENTER

10

SOUTH GATE

710

WATTS TOWERS

105

LYNWOOD

ANGELS FLIGHT

BRADBURY BUILDING

CALIFORNIA SCIENCE CENTER

CENTRAL LIBRARY

CITY HALL

FASHION DISTRICT

GRAND CENTRAL MARKET

GRAND PARK FOUNTAIN

LITTLE TOKYO

NATURAL HISTORY MUSEUM

OLVERA STREET

LA LIVE

THE LAST BOOKSTORE

UNION STATION

WALT DISNEY CONCERT HALL

WATTS TOWERS

# ANGELS FLIGHT RAILWAY

**TOP ENTRANCE:**
CALIFORNIA PLAZA, 350 SOUTH GRAND AVENUE,
LOS ANGELES 90071

**THE LOWER ENTRANCE:**
351 SOUTH HILL STREET, LOS ANGELES 90013

Angels Flight opened in 1901 as a way for Angelenos to get up and down Bunker Hill in Downtown Los Angeles, and it's known as the world's shortest railway. Technically a funicular, Angels Flight is made up of 2 cars that run side by side, in opposition to each other; meaning when one is up the other is down. It's a delightful thing to do with kids, for the entire 3 minutes the ride takes, and if you ride from top to bottom, you'll be dropped off across the street from Grand Central Market.

# BRADBURY BUILDING

304 S. BROADWAY, LOS ANGELES, CA 90013

Recognized as the oldest commercial building in
downtown L.A., the Bradbury Building is not like most
buildings we find ourselves in today. Here you'll find
marble stairs, open-cage elevators, iron railings, and a
light-filled Victorian court. Kids who are intrigued with
building and design will most likely appreciate this
often-photographed building. It is a National Historic
Landmark and has been featured in many movies and
television shows, like "Blade Runner."

## CALIFORNIA SCIENCE CENTER
### 700 EXPOSITION PARK DR, Los Angeles, CA 90037

The California Science Center is one of the best kid-friendly museums in Los Angeles, and it's one of the best Science Museums in California overall! There are plenty of things for kids to do, touch, and experience first-hand. All the exhibits encourage kids to ask questions and find out answers about "how" and "why" things are the way they are. And don't miss seeing the Space Shuttle Endeavour while you're there - or consider seeing an IMAX movie in their theater.

*↙ Space Shuttle !*

5

# CENTRAL LIBRARY
## 630 W. 5TH STREET, LOS ANGELES, CA 90071

The Central Library isn't your average public library. For starters, it's huge – as public libraries go. And, it almost serves as a type of museum because of the different art and architectural styles on display. You'll find examples of Art Deco pieces, an astounding Rotunda, sculptures, murals, and more. A ride in the elevators won't just take you from floor to floor, but will also give you the chance to teach your children about card catalogs; the inside of the elevators are papered with them. You'll find the Children's

Literature Department on level 2 of the Goodhue Building. In addition to the thousands of items available for loan, you'll also find a wide assortment of activities and programs that are all offered free of charge.

## CITY HALL
### 200 N. SPRING STREET, Los Angeles, CA 90012

Los Angeles City Hall is where the Mayor's office is and where the City Council meets, and much of the building is open to the public. This beautiful building will appeal to those who love to see art deco designs, and even if that's not your thing, the 27th floor observation deck is worth the trip. You'll get an amazing view of Downtown Los Angeles from on high, and if the weather cooperates, you can see all the way to the ocean.

## FASHION DISTRICT
### MULTIPLE BLOCKS AROUND SANTEE AND OLYMPIC IN DTLA

Fashion, Flowers, Fabric and Food - you'll find all that and more in The LA Fashion District in Downtown Los Angeles. Whether you're looking for a Quinceañera dress in Santee Alley, searching for luxury fabric, or shopping for the best prices for wedding flowers in the LA flower district shops, you won't be disappointed. It's fun to take the kids for back-to-school shopping and grab a bite to eat.

# GRAND CENTRAL MARKET

## 317 S BROADWAY, LOS ANGELES, CA 90013

For almost 100 years, the Grand Central Market has been bringing our city's diverse cultures and food to one location. Get ready to be on sensory overload — the sights, the smells, the tastes contained within this 30,000-foot space. You'll find food from all corners of the world, coffee, juice, ice cream, flowers, and more. Even a picky eater can find something to eat here, and the portions are huge!

# GRAND PARK AND FOUNTAIN

## 200 N GRAND AVE, LOS ANGELES, CA 90012

A splash pad is a terrific invention for a hot day. Kids are delighted by random water jets, can get a little bit wet, and have a ton of fun, but you don't need to pack a beach bag or find a pool. Also, there's no need to know how to swim, so it's just fun. The beautiful fountain and splash pad in Grand Park also offer views of

City Hall as a bonus. Plus, Grand Park itself is the site of many festivals and big events.

## LITTLE TOKYO
### Los Angeles 90012

Little Tokyo is one of only three official Japantowns within the United States, and offers many ways for families to learn about a culture they may not be familiar with, have some fun, and gain some knowledge. Try a Self-Guided Walking tour of Little Tokyo Historic District, or visit the Japanese American National Museum.

## NATURAL HISTORY MUSEUM
### 900 W EXPOSITION BLVD, Los Angeles, CA 90007

The Natural History Museum is one of those museums that offers something for everyone. Their permanent exhibits include Dinosaur Hall (where you can see a trio of more than 2,000 specimens of gems and minerals from around the world), the outdoors Nature Gar-

dens, the Animal Habitat Halls (featuring impressive dioramas), and much more. And while many parts of the museum are hands-off, there are also sections that are entirely interactive and very kid-friendly. Be sure to visit the Hall of Birds (featuring interactive exhibits), the Discovery Center (complete with microscopes, touchable fossils and furs, and a polar bear collected in Norway back in 1964), and the Nature Lab (giving kids a hands-on sense of the nature surrounding us on a daily basis).

# OLVERA STREET
## Los Angeles, CA 90012

Olvera Street, El Pueblo de Los Angeles, is known as the birthplace of Los Angeles. Visit this lively outdoor marketplace and enjoy a variety of vendors, dancers and musicians, handcrafted items, and delicious food. Families can explore on their own or take advantage of free docent-led tours of Olvera Street and El Pueblo de Los Angeles Historical Monument. There are many festivals and special events held here throughout the year.

# LA LIVE
## 800 WEST OLYMPIC BLVD., Los Angeles 90015

LA Live is a Sports and Entertainment hub in downtown Los Angeles, with the Crypto.com arena, home to the Lakers and Kings, the Microsoft Theater and Regal Cinemas, as well as more than a dozen restaurants, and right next door to the LA Convention Center. There's always something exciting happening, like when the outdoor ice rink appears for the Holidays, or when there's a concert or big game.

# THE LAST BOOKSTORE
## 453 SOUTH SPRING STREET, Los Angeles, CA 90013

Make sure kids know that books aren't just bought from Amazon, and take them to The Last Bookstore,

California's largest new and used book store. They occupy 20,000 square feet of space and feature more than two hundred thousand books! In addition, you and your kids will marvel at the many "extras," including a "tunnel" made out of books.

## UNION STATION
### 800 N ALAMEDA ST, Los Angeles, CA 90012

Union Station is part of LA's history, and it's a really fun place to explore with kids. You're sure to see beautiful tile work, fountains, and you will probably feel like you've seen everything in a movie before - because you have. Union Station has been in many movies, TV

shows, and commercials over the years. There's also terrific public art both in Union Station itself and across the tracks in the Metro station.

## WALT DISNEY CONCERT HALL
III S GRAND AVE, Los ANGELEs, CA 90012

Take Kids for a special show, or even just a tour! The Walt Disney Concert Hall is the home of the LA Philharmonic, and has become one of the most iconic buildings in downtown Los Angeles, and was designed by Frank Gehry. Self-guided tours are available. And if your kids want to see a show, there are dozens of family-friendly performances held all year long.

## WATTS TOWERS
### 1727 E 107TH ST, LOS ANGELES, CA 90002

The Watts Towers are truly a sight to see. A visual representation that dreams can become a reality. The Watts Towers are constructed of a structural steel core, wrapped in wire mesh which has been covered with mortar, and inlaid with tiles, glass, shell, pottery, and rocks. The tallest of the towers stands at 99.5 feet. The Watts Towers stand "as a symbol of freedom, creativity, and initiative." The artist, Simon Rodia, originally called his creation "Nuestro Pueblo," or "our town." These towers were built by hand, by a guy in his backyard, essentially, and have become one of the iconic symbols of Los Angeles. Simon Rodia's story is amazing and the Watts Towers are a must-see. *(And yes, they're in Watts, not technically in downtown, but nearby.)*

14

# HOLLYWOOD & GRIFFITH PARK

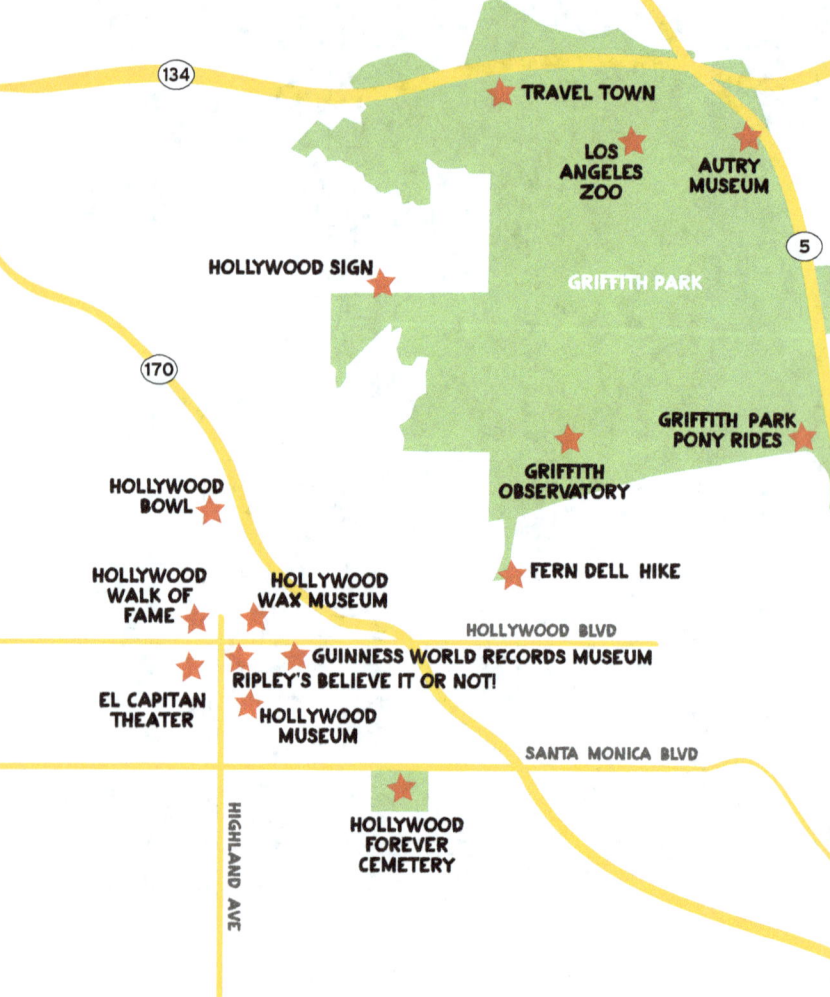

134

TRAVEL TOWN

LOS ANGELES ZOO

AUTRY MUSEUM

5

HOLLYWOOD SIGN

GRIFFITH PARK

170

GRIFFITH PARK PONY RIDES

GRIFFITH OBSERVATORY

HOLLYWOOD BOWL

HOLLYWOOD WALK OF FAME

HOLLYWOOD WAX MUSEUM

FERN DELL HIKE

HOLLYWOOD BLVD

GUINNESS WORLD RECORDS MUSEUM

RIPLEY'S BELIEVE IT OR NOT!

EL CAPITAN THEATER

HOLLYWOOD MUSEUM

SANTA MONICA BLVD

HIGHLAND AVE

HOLLYWOOD FOREVER CEMETERY

AUTRY MUSEUM OF THE AMERICAN WEST

EL CAPITAN THEATER

FERN DELL HIKE

GRIFFITH PARK PONY RIDES

GRIFFITH OBSERVATORY

GUINNESS WORLD RECORDS MUSEUM

HOLLYWOOD BOWL

HOLLYWOOD FOREVER CEMETERY

HOLLYWOOD MUSEUM

HOLLYWOOD SIGN

HOLLYWOOD WALK OF FAME

HOLLYWOOD WAX MUSEUM

LOS ANGELES ZOO

RIPLEY'S BELIEVE IT OR NOT!

TRAVEL TOWN MUSEUM

# AUTRY MUSEUM OF THE AMERICAN WEST

## 4700 WESTERN HERITAGE WAY, LOS ANGELES, CA 90027

The Autry Museum celebrates the history, art, and culture of the American West. The Museum is home to a number of permanent exhibits that help visitors get a sense of how things have changed (and remained the same) over the years. The Autry is considered to be the only museum of its kind that combines Western history and cultures with Native American perspectives. The Autry also offers a number of family-friendly and inter-active activities. Kids will have fun learning how movie sound effects are made, panning for "gold," sitting on top of a mock-up of a horse (in front of a screen) and pretending to ride along in a western film!

# EL CAPITAN THEATER

## 6838 HOLLYWOOD BLVD., LOS ANGELES, CA 90028

Originally opened in 1926, the El Capitan has been restored to provide all who come a completely enchant-ing movie-going experience. In addition to state-of-the-art cinematic technology, the El Capitan also usually includes pre-show entertainment as well as prop and/or costume exhibits. It is also an exclusive first run theatre for Walt Disney Pictures which means you can look forward to Star Wars, Pixar, Marvel, and of course Disney movies screening here.

## FERN DELL HIKE, GRIFFITH PARK
### FERN DELL DR, LOS ANGELES, CA 90027

If you're looking for a short hike, especially on a hot day, Fern Dell is a great choice. You may feel like you've entered a tropical forest, even though you're still in Griffith Park, as you walk among California sycamores and tropical plants, and count more than 50 different fern species, some native plants and some not. The trail is only half a mile long, but it's a delightful experience for all ages. It's shaded and flat enough to use a stroller easily. There's a stream running through the dell, which is fed by a natural spring, and the ponds and little waterfalls it forms keep the place cool and inviting. The walking path takes you over several bridges, perfect for watching the water go by, and for delighting and engaging the kids! If you time it right, you'll be able to stop at the Trails Cafe, located along the path, and enjoy a slice of pie and a cold drink, or other snacks from their menu. It's a little oasis within the park and there are tables and a play area nearby. Griffith Park is overall a wonderful place to experience with kids. There are many, many things to do in this 4000-acre Park.

## GRIFFITH PARK PONY RIDES

### 4400 CRYSTAL SPRINGS DR., LOS ANGELES, CA 90027

Let the kids channel their inner cowboy and cowgirl at the Griffith Park Pony Rides, which has been in business since 1948. For a small price per ride, children can choose from slow, medium, or fast ponies. (Age and weight restrictions apply). As an added bonus, there's a petting zoo on select days and they also host birthday parties.

## GRIFFITH OBSERVATORY

### 2800 E. OBSERVATORY RD., LOS ANGELES, CA 90027

The Griffith Observatory brings the wonder of outer space in a family-friendly, accessible way. There are telescopes and a multitude of exhibits that will keep the kids (and parents) engaged, curious, and in awe. And on clear days, you'll enjoy great views of Los Angeles and the Hollywood sign! There is a cafe on site as well. (Outside food and drinks are not permitted inside the Observatory). Admission to the Observatory, and parking, are free—although there is a fee for shows in the Samuel Oschin Planetarium.

## GUINNESS WORLD RECORDS MUSEUM

### 6764 HOLLYWOOD BLVD., HOLLYWOOD, CA 90028

It's where the Guinness World Record Books come to life. Stroll around and compare your height to that of the world's tallest person (just one fun fact you'll encounter). Check out the unique and the unusual in a fun, interactive way. The website even has a special "Youth Materials" section with printables  that kids can either complete while they walk through the museum or before their visit.

## HOLLYWOOD BOWL

### 2301 N HIGHLAND AVE, Los Angeles, CA 90068

For many families, it isn't summer without attending a Hollywood Bowl concert. The Bowl opened in 1922 and since that time this world-famous venue has showcased a variety of musical talents ranging from The Beatles to Ella Fitzgerald to Stevie Wonder to John Williams. During the summer, the Bowl hosts "Classical Tuesday and Thursdays" with the Los Angeles Philharmonic, Jazz at the Bowl, Weekend Spectaculars, KCRW's World Festival, Sunday Sunset Concerts, and Special Concerts.

# HOLLYWOOD FOREVER CEMETERY
## 6000 SANTA MONICA BLVD., LOS ANGELES, CA 90038

Hollywood Forever is not just a cemetery, it's a hub for events like the annual Día de los Muertos celebration they host every November. The event features vendors (arts and crafts and food), more than 100 altars created by the community, hundreds of Aztec Ritual Dancers, five stages featuring music and theatrical performances, a costume contest, and more. There are also numerous family-friendly concerts and movie screenings throughout the year.

# HOLLYWOOD MUSEUM
## 1660 N. HIGHLAND AVE., HOLLYWOOD, CA 90028

Located within the Historic Max Factor Museum, the Hollywood Museum features four floors that are home to more than 10,000 items. You'll find photographs, props, costumes, memorabilia, posters, and more all from favorite movies and TV shows.

# HOLLYWOOD SIGN
## LOS ANGELES, CA 90068

If you've got family visiting from out-of-town, a hike to see the famous Hollywood Sign may be in order. One available route starts at the Griffith Observatory, another route (longer and steeper) is closer to the Greek

Theatre. Make sure to wear appropriate shoes and sunscreen, and have water with you. And get ready to take the best selfie ever.

## HOLLYWOOD WALK OF FAME

### HOLLYWOOD BLVD BETWEEN LA BREA AND GOWER AND ON VINE STREET FROM SUNSET TO YUCCA 90028

We are in the entertainment capital of the world, after all, and one of the tourist-y things to do that you must do as a local at least once - is walk along the Hollywood Walk of Fame. For the unini- tiated, the Walk of Fame is the sidewalk of Hollywood Blvd., where brass-outlined stars have been embedded into the walkway. Stars from present day and from ages past can be found - and it's a test to see how

many you can place. Plus you'll get to see a cast of characters and character impersonators busking and ready to pose for photos. Like nowhere else.

## HOLLYWOOD WAX MUSEUM

6767 HOLLYWOOD BLVD., Los ANGELES, CA 90028

The Hollywood Wax Museum is the longest running wax museum in the United States. Open every day of the year, it's a fun way to mingle and pose among the stars! Grab your phones and start snapping some fun selfies with a wide variety of celebrities.

## LOS ANGELES ZOO

5333 ZOO DRIVE, Los ANGELES, CA 90027

Set on 133 acres, you'll find more than 1,000 mammals, birds, amphibians, and reptiles at the L.A. Zoo! Among some of the exhibits you'll explore, you'll find the new Rainforest of the Americas, the Elephants of Asia habitat, the Campo Gorilla Reserve, the LAIR (Living Amphibians, Invertebrates, and Reptiles), the Sea Life Cliffs, and more. There's also the Winnick

Family Children's Zoo. Families may bring their own picnics or purchase food from several spots throughout the Zoo.

## RIPLEY'S BELIEVE IT OR NOT!

6780 HOLLYWOOD BLVD., HOLLYWOOD 90028

The World is filled with some strange and interesting things, but most of us don't usually experience them in our daily lives. Ripley's Believe it or Not! has been curating a collection of unusual things for years and they're on display here in their "Odditorium"

for you and your kids to see and marvel at. Fair warning that some of the items on display may be considered disturbing; please check before going.

## TRAVEL TOWN MUSEUM
**5200 ZOO DRIVE, GRIFFITH PARK, LOS ANGELES, CA 90027**

Families visiting Travel Town Museum in Griffith Park will find so much to do and explore including a collection of locomotives and passenger cars dating back to the 1800s. Travel Town is an outdoor museum which preserves and celebrates the railroad heritage of the western United States through  its history and its artifacts. Travel Town is *the* place to visit if you have train-lovers in your family. The spot was developed in the 1950s and features an impressive collection of locomotives, freight cars, cabooses, and passenger cars.

# Westside
## & ALONG the COAST

TOPANGA CANYON
HORSEBACK RIDING

WILL GEER
THEATRICUM
BOTANICUM

WILL ROGERS
STATE PARK

TOPANGA
STATE PARK

UCLA

RODEO DRIVE
BEVERLY HILLS

MALIBU
BEACHES

TEMESCAL
GATEWAY
PARK

MALIBU
CREEK

ADAMSON
HOUSE

PALISADES
PARK

DOUGLAS
PARK

405

110

10

ANNENBERG
PALISADES PARK &
CAMERA OBSCURA

SANTA MONICA PIER

VENICE BEACH

VENICE CANALS

TONGVA PARK

BALDWIN HILLS
OVERLOOK

STAR ECO STATION

MOTHER'S BEACH

LAX

MARINA
DEL REY

105

105

EL SEGUNDO

MANHATTAN
BEACH

405

REDONDO
BEACH

110

LONG
BEACH

AQUARIUM
OF THE
PACIFIC

RANCHO
PALOS VERDES

BATTLESHIP IOWA

KOREAN
FRIENSHIP
BELL

SAN
PEDRO

SANTA
CATALINA
ISLAND

CABRILLO
MARINE AQUARIUM

ADAMSON HOUSE

ANNENBERG COMMUNITY BEACH HOUSE

AQUARIUM OF THE PACIFIC

BALDWIN HILLS SCENIC OVERLOOK

BATTLESHIP IOWA IN SAN PEDRO

CABRILLO MARINE AQUARIUM

CATALINA ISLAND

DOUGLAS PARK SANTA MONICA

KOREAN FRIENDSHIP BELL

MALIBU BEACHES

MALIBU CREEK STATE PARK

MOTHER'S BEACH MARINA DEL REY

PALISADES PARK + CAMERA OBSCURA

SANTA MONICA PIER

STAR ECO STATION

TEMESCAL GATEWAY CANYON HIKE

THEATRICUM BOTANICUM

TONGVA PARK SANTA MONICA

TOPANGA CANYON HORSEBACK RIDING

UCLA CAMPUS

VENICE BEACH AND BOARDWALK, VENICE
CANALS, AND VENICE SKATE PARK

WILL ROGERS STATE PARK

# ADAMSON HOUSE

The Adamson House is a great place to take the family for a little day trip R & R. It's right in our SoCal backyard, but it feels like you've left the 'burbs and are really exploring California's historic coastline. The house was built by the family who owned the last Malibu Spanish Land Grant and who went on to own the famous Malibu Potteries factory. Now a State Park, a National Historic Site and a California Historical Landmark, Adamson House is located where the Malibu Creek flows into the Pacific Ocean. The setting is quite idyllic and it can be rented out for special occasions, so you may see wedding photos being taken when you visit.

# ANNENBERG COMMUNITY BEACH HOUSE

415 PACIFIC COAST HIGHWAY, SANTA MONICA, CA 90402

Located at Santa Monica State Beach, the Annenberg Community Beach House is a spectacular 5-acre property with a rich history. The site was once a 110-room mansion built for Marion Davies by William Randolph Hearst. Transformed by generous donations, the Beach House is open to the community, does not require membership, and offers a splash pad, children's play area and pool, as well as event space, and access to the

fabulous Santa Monica Beach. A small cafe is located on-site as well. The Annenberg also hosts a variety of classes and community activities throughout the year.

## AQUARIUM OF THE PACIFIC

### 100 AQUARIUM WAY, LONG BEACH, CA 90802

You'll find so much to see and do at the Aquarium of the Pacific in Long Beach. In addition to having thousands of animal exhibits, a shark lagoon and penguin habitat, families will find a fun special event almost every weekend or holiday. The new wing houses the state-of-the-art immersive Honda Pacific Visions Theater, features interactive exhibi-

tions, an art gallery that transports visitors under the ocean, and live animal exhibits, all intended to showcase the most pressing environmental issues of our time and help explore alternative pathways to designing a more sustainable future.

## BALDWIN HILLS SCENIC OVERLOOK
### 6300 HETZLER RD., CULVER CITY, CA 90232

Look at Los Angeles in a different way, say from the top of a 500 foot peak by enjoying a family hike at the Baldwin Hills Scenic Overlook, also known as the "Culver City Stairs." (Be prepared that little ones may tire out and ask to be carried). You'll wander through a restored native habitat and be able to examine exhibits at the visitor center (which is open on weekends.) It's a steep climb to the top (on stairs) so be prepared.

## BATTLESHIP IOWA IN SAN PEDRO
### 250 S. HARBOR BLVD., SAN PEDRO, CA 90731

A visit to San Pedro wouldn't be complete without a visit to the Battleship IOWA. This battleship is in fact an interactive naval museum. Families can take a self-guided tour and get a sense of what life was like for our country's sailors. Known as the "Battle-

ship of Presidents," the IOWA served our country for over 50 years. In addition, special attention has been made to make sure that the youngest visitors are engaged in their visit. There's even a special "Victory the Dog Adventure" scavenger hunt for kids.

## RODEO DRIVE IN BEVERLY HILLS
### BETWEEN WILSHIRE BLVD AND SANTA MONICA BLVD., BEVERLY HILLS 90212

Rodeo Drive is famous for the high-end luxury shops that line both sides of the blocks. You can window shop for hours, and try to catch a glimpse of celebrities as they head into the fancy stores - and of course you can head inside, too! Be sure to visit at Holiday time, when the street is decorated,

but it's always a lovely place to visit. There are lots of restaurants to choose from when the strolling makes you hungry, and the City of Beverly Hills offers multiple spots with free 2-hour parking.

## CABRILLO MARINE AQUARIUM
### 3720 STEPHEN M. WHITE DR., SAN PEDRO, CA 90731

Kids will certainly enjoy a visit to the Cabrillo Marine Aquarium. The Aquarium houses a large collection of Southern California marine life. Inside the 21,000 square-foot Frank Gehry-designed facility, you'll find an auditorium, an Aquatic Nursery, an outdoor tide pool touch tank, a teaching laboratory, an Exploration Center, and more. The Aquarium also hosts a variety of special events throughout the year.

## CATALINA ISLAND
### CATALINA, CA 90704

Catalina Island is an ideal spot to have fun with your family, with dozens of activities to suit any budget: from lounging on the sand and splashing in the waves for free, to renting a kayak, taking a glass-bottom boat ride, ziplining through the canyons, getting an off-road jeep tour of the Island's interior, playing a round of golf (regular-sized or mini), or even–*gulp*–parasailing. You can even get into a Biofuel H1 Hummer with 10 of your newest best friends and a Guide and head off on

a dirt road into what is the majority of Catalina Island
– wilderness. 47,000 acres, to be exact, are what
have been preserved as the Catalina Island Conser-
vancy and are to remain untouched by development
for all time. Kids often are fascinated that there are so
few cars allowed on the Island, and that most people
get around in golf carts (or on foot).

### DOUGLAS PARK SANTA MONICA
#### 2439 WILSHIRE BLVD., SANTA MONICA, CA

Kids will find plenty to keep themselves happy and
entertained at this relatively small park. Douglas Park
features a man-made creek, picnic tables, tennis courts,
reflecting pools, a playground, and a splash pad.
Have kids take a look and see how many different
types of animals they can find!

# KOREAN BELL OF FRIENDSHIP

## ANGELS GATE PARK
### 3601 S. GAFFEY ST., SAN PEDRO, CA 90731

The Korean Bell of Friendship was donated by the Republic of Korea in 1976, in honor of our country's bicentennial. It honors Korean War veterans as well as serving as a symbol of friendship between our two countries. The Korean Bell weighs 17 tons and stands 12 feet tall. Four times a year (on the 4th of July, August 15th (Korean Independence Day), New Year's Eve, and in September to celebrate Constitution Week, the bell is struck with a wooden log. The bell is inside a pagoda-like structure which was constructed in San Pedro by 30 craftsmen who were flown in from Korea. In addition, the Korean Bell of Friendship is located in a picturesque setting — perfect for a picnic or for flying a kite, because it gets breezy!

## MALIBU BEACHES
### 7103 WESTWARD BEACH ROAD, MALIBU, CA 90265

You have to visit the beaches in Malibu, since they're all amazing and it's a quintessentially Southern California thing to do. Whether you choose to explore Zuma Beach, Malibu Surfrider Beach, or Point Dume State Beach, you'll be rewarded with a beautiful coastline and fun family times. And you never know - you might just see a celebrity resident or two paddling out to ride the waves.

## MALIBU CREEK STATE PARK
### 1925 LAS VIRGENES ROAD, CALABASAS, CA 91302

Families can enjoy horseback riding, swimming, hiking, fishing, and more at this amazing spot. Camping amenities include fire rings and showers. Malibu Creek

State Park has also served as the filming location for television shows over the years including *M*A*S*H* and *Planet of the Apes.*

## MOTHER'S BEACH

4101 ADMIRALTY WAY, MARINA DEL REY, CA 90292

Locals call it "Mother's Beach," because this beach is a good spot to bring young children to, without any worry of large waves. Here you'll find a children's playground, picnic tables, and "gentle beach access" so kids can splash and play. Once upon a time, the water was considered too polluted for most Moms to want to take their kids, but after years of effort, the county of LA has built filtering mechanisms that have cleaned up the water. Heal the Bay rates it an A. Enjoy!

## PALISADES PARK AND CAMERA OBSCURA

### ADJACENT TO OCEAN AVENUE, BETWEEN COLORADO AVENUE AND ADELAIDE DRIVE

Palisades Park is a 1.5 mile stretch of park and walkways along a 100-foot cliff overlooking the Pacific Ocean. You'll have unobstructed views to the West, as far as the eye can see, as you stroll along with your kids. Scattered throughout this park are fun things to look at and play on, including public art installations like the Beacon Overlook, the Gestation III wooden sculpture, which is great for kids to climb on and in, and the famous Camera Obscura. Take your kids inside for some mind-blowing visuals that you can tell them were discovered with technology that was invented—*gasp*—before the Internet.

## SANTA MONICA PIER

### 200 SANTA MONICA PIER, SANTA MONICA 90401

### AT THE VERY END OF COLORADO BLVD AND THE PACIFIC OCEAN

Super family friendly and perfect for all ages, the iconic Santa Monica Pier is the historic landmark known far and wide as a symbol of Southern Cal-

ifornia. The pier itself dates back to 1909, and marks the Western end of famed Route 66. The pier is home to Pacific Park amusement park, including a giant ferris wheel, rides, and games. There's also a family-friendly Carousel, a small aquarium run by Heal the Bay, and multiple dining options as well. The Pier is the site of many festivals throughout the year, including a Summer concert series and outdoor movies.

## STAR ECO STATION
### 10101 JEFFERSON BLVD., CULVER CITY, CA 90232

The STAR Eco Station is the place to bring kids who are interested in animals and their role in making sure these animals are safe. Partly a museum and partly an exotic wildlife rescue facility, the STAR Eco Station is a special place. Here you'll find animals that you won't find anywhere else. Families will participate in hands-on ecology lessons and be able to observe a variety of birds, reptiles, and mammals. They hold many special events throughout the year, and they also host a Summer Camp.

## TEMESCAL GATEWAY CANYON HIKE
### 15601 SUNSET BLVD., PACIFIC PALISADES, CA

Temescal Gateway Park includes 141 acres. You'll find picnic tables, hiking trails, and large grassy areas here. Hiking through the park will give your family an appreciation of nature and reward you with some incredible views. If you do go hiking, be on the lookout for **Skull Rock** — a sandstone formation that some say resembles a skull. As a bonus, parking is generally easy to find here.

## THEATRICUM BOTANICUM
### 1419 N. TOPANGA CANYON BLVD., TOPANGA, CA 90290

Actor Will Geer founded the Theatricum Botanicum in 1973. Since then, families have been enjoying plays and education programs in this one-of-a-kind outdoor setting. The 299-seat amphitheater offers a variety of special programs.

# TONGVA PARK

1615 OCEAN AVE., SANTA MONICA, CA 90401

6-acre Tongva Park was once an asphalt parking lot. Now, families will find a pleasant park divided into four sections – Observation Hill, Discovery Hill, Garden Hill, and Gathering Hill. In the Discovery Hill section, families will find a children's play area and shaded picnic areas. Gathering Hills is the site of a grassy amphitheater where the city hosts a variety of free performances. The name, Tongva Park, honors the indigenous Tongva people who once lived in the region for thousands of years.

# TOPANGA CANYON HORSEBACK RIDING

2623 OLD TOPANGA CANYON ROAD, TOPANGA, CA 90290

Enjoy an outdoor adventure with your family and head out to Los Angeles Horseback Riding in Topanga Canyon. Riders of all experience levels are welcome, but keep in mind that children must be at least six years old to ride these horses, and are required to wear helmets. You'll enjoy both mountain and ocean views as you ride. Be sure to check the website for an important list of what is and isn't allowed (long pants and closed-toe shoes are both required). Advance reservations are required, and a variety of packages are offered so you can select the ride that is best for your family.

## UCLA CAMPUS

WESTWOOD, LOS ANGELES
90095

Let's face it: you probably
want your kid to go to UCLA
one day - or you went there
- or you wish you did. One of the best Universities in
the world is right in our midst, and whether you have
Bruin aspirations or not, it's a beautiful campus to walk
around. Located right on Campus is the Fowler Museum, and the Mildred E. Mathias Botanical Garden,
both of which are terrific places to take the kids, and
The Hammer Museum is just down the street. After-
wards, Westwood is a terrific place to grab a bite and
stroll, either longing for those college days, planning
ahead for your kids', or being glad they're done.

## VENICE BEACH AND BOARDWALK,
## VENICE CANALS,
## AND VENICE SKATE PARK

1800 OCEAN FRONT WALK, LOS ANGELES 90291

You're never quite sure what you may see while strolling along the 2-mile long Venice Beach Boardwalk,
but you certainly won't be bored! You'll find a number
of street performers, vendors, art pieces, restaurants

and refreshment stands, and souvenir shops here. Plus you're steps from the sand! There's a bike path that runs for miles along the coast, so you can bring your bikes or rent a set for the day. If you've got skateboarders (or skateboarding fans) in the family, then you've got to hang out at the Venice Skate Park. Located right next to the beach, this 16,000 square foot space is ideal for both beginners and more experienced skaters to show off their moves. And it wouldn't be a day in Venice if you didn't also head over to the nearby Venice Canals,

where you'll get to see the waterways constructed back in the early 1900s by Abbot Kinney, part of his grand vision for "the Venice of America."

## WILL ROGERS STATE PARK

1501 WILL ROGERS PARK RD., PACIFIC PALISADES, CA 90272

Will Rogers was a popular actor in the 1930s, who gained fame as a columnist, radio personality, and movie star. He enjoyed horseback riding and roping, and purchased his Ranch in order to keep his horses and spend time with family. After his death, the land was donated to California and became the Will Rogers State Historic Park. Guided tours of the ranch house are offered at select times, or for families who prefer, they can explore the ranch on a self-guided tour. The Visitor Center offers exhibits about the history of the site. There is also a hiking trail here which will lead you up to Inspiration Point, and a Polo field where you can watch a match. The great lawn is an ideal spot for a family picnic.

# *Points East* →

**CASTLE PARK**
**DESCANSO GARDENS**
**FIESTA VILLAGE FAMILY FUN PARK**
**FRANK G. BONELLI PARK BOATING IN SAN DIMAS**
**HUNTINGTON LIBRARY AND GARDENS**

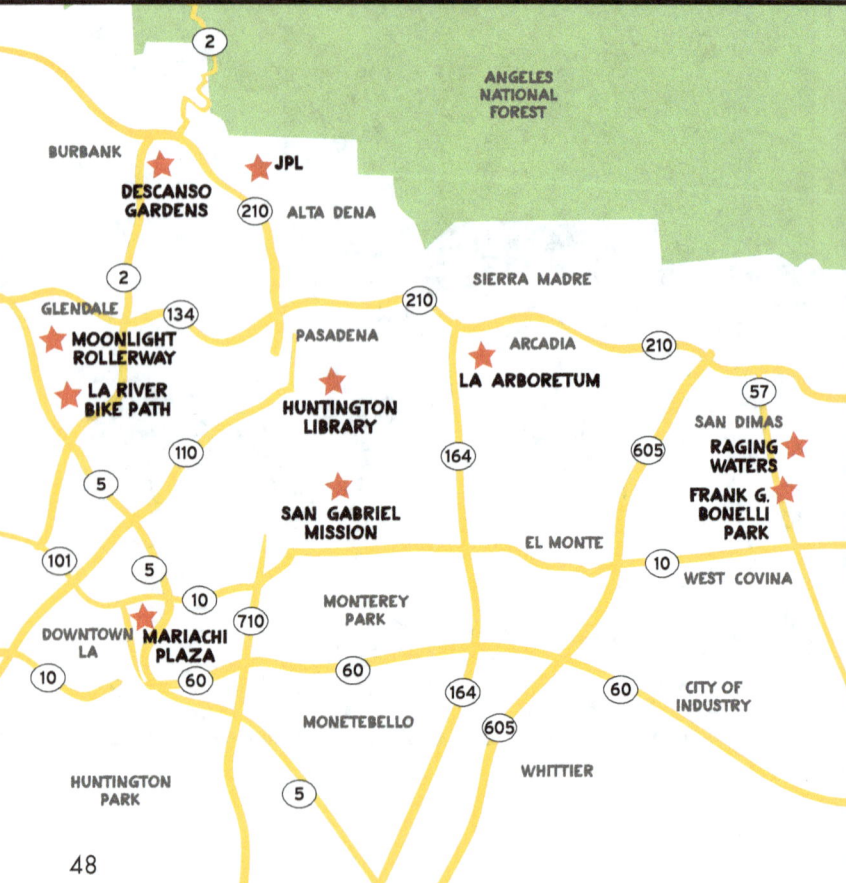

ANGELES
NATIONAL
FOREST

BURBANK

② JPL

DESCANSO
GARDENS

②⑩ ALTA DENA

SIERRA MADRE

② ⑩

GLENDALE ⑬④

MOONLIGHT
ROLLERWAY

PASADENA

ARCADIA ②⑩

LA ARBORETUM

LA RIVER
BIKE PATH

HUNTINGTON
LIBRARY

SAN DIMAS

RAGING
WATERS

⑪⓪ ⑥⓪⑤

⑤ ⑯④

FRANK G.
BONELLI
PARK

SAN GABRIEL
MISSION

EL MONTE

⑩① ⑤ ⑩

⑩ WEST COVINA

⑦⑩ MONTEREY
PARK

DOWNTOWN
LA MARIACHI
PLAZA

⑩ ⑥⓪

⑥⓪

⑯④

⑥⓪ CITY OF
INDUSTRY

MONETEBELLO

⑥⓪⑤

HUNTINGTON
PARK

⑤

WHITTIER

48

JET PROPULSION LAB (JPL)
LOGAN'S CANDIES
LOS ANGELES COUNTY ARBORETUM
LOS ANGELES RIVER CENTER AND BIKE PATH
MARCH FIELD AIR MUSEUM
MARIACHI PLAZA
MOONLIGHT ROLLERWAY
MISSION INN AND MUSEUM
PALM SPRINGS
PLANES OF FAME MUSEUM
RAGING WATERS
SAN GABRIEL MISSION

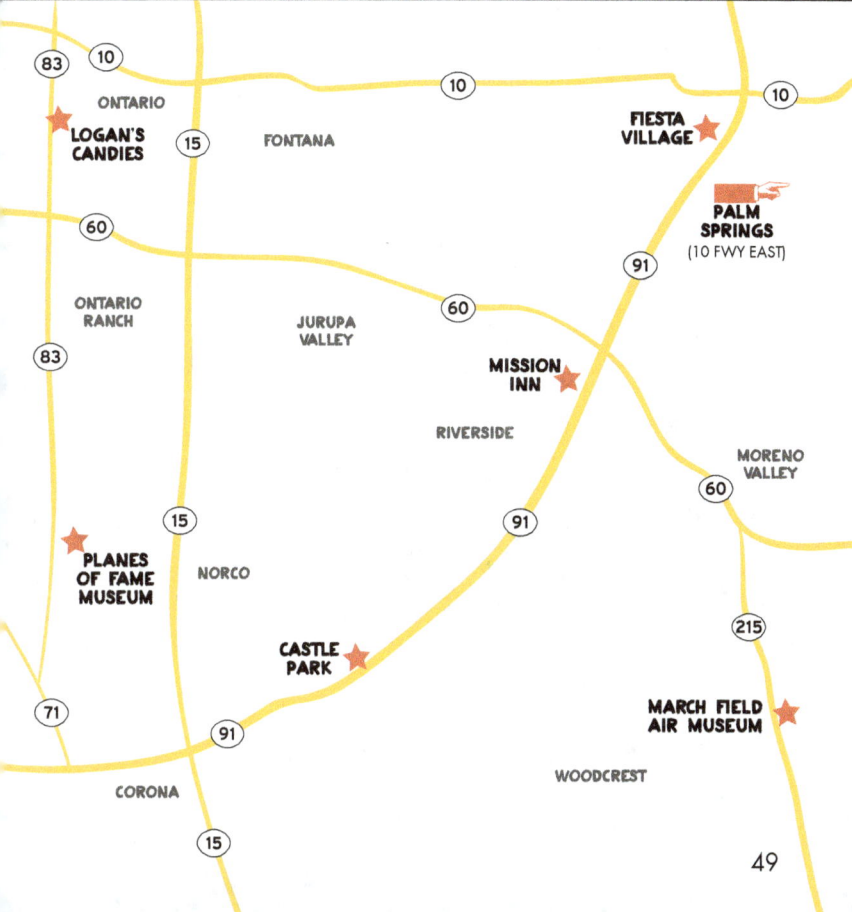

## CASTLE PARK

### 3500 POLK ST., RIVERSIDE, CA 92505

Castle Park is a popular amusement park, founded in 1976, and spread out over 25 acres. Families will find over 25 rides and attractions here, as well as four 18-hole miniature golf courses, a video arcade, carnival games, a water park called Buccaneer Cove, and more. It's like the carnival came to town and never left! Rides include the Tilt a Whirl, Scrambler, a Merry-Go-Round, Bumper Cars, and roller coasters that will satisfy even the biggest thrill seekers. Bringing the little ones with you? Not to worry; there are several rides that are suitable for toddlers. Buccaneer Cove has five water slides, water tunnels and lots of water sprays - along with plenty of shade to cool off on the hottest days. There are even Cabanas for rent. On top of that, Castle Park puts on an awesome Magic Show every day.

# DESCANSO GARDENS

## 1418 DESCANSO DRIVE, LA CAÑADA FLINTRIDGE, CA 91011

Descanso Gardens is an urban retreat of year-round natural beauty, and internationally renowned botanical collections with spectacular seasonal horticultural displays. Visit for a stroll, a concert, or a class—there are so many ways to explore. The Enchanted Railroad is a treat for families - a small, life-like train that can carry both adults and kids around the gardens. And they often host a special holiday event.

# FIESTA VILLAGE

## 1405 E WASHINGTON ST, COLTON, CA 92324

You could stay all day and probably not do all the fun things at Fiesta Village Family Fun Park, but why not try? Let's start with Laser Tag, which is fun for all ages. Then there are the rides, like Tilt-a-Whirl, Bizzy Bears, Slugger's Super Slide, and The Scrambler. Mini-golf? There are two courses, so don't worry about waiting in long lines. What about working on your swing at the batting cages? Yes, they have those, too! If you're into roller skating or roller blading, try out their enormous outdoor skating rink, complete with rentals available if you forgot yours at home. Fiesta Raceway is the place to have fun Go-Kart racing along the winding, well-maintained and well-supervised track. As if that weren't enough, there's also a water park! Pyrite Rapids Water Park is a blast, and a perfect way to cool off in the hot Summer months.

## FRANK G. BONELLI PARK
### 120 VIA VERDE PARK RD., SAN DIMAS, CA 91773

The Frank G. Bonelli Regional Park isn't your run-of-the-mill neighborhood park. Within this 1,800-acre facility you'll find a 250-acre lake (Puddingstone Lake), 14 miles of multi-use trails, and more. It's the perfect spot for nature walks, hiking, family picnics, swimming, jet skiing, and boating.

## HUNTINGTON LIBRARY AND GARDENS
### 1151 OXFORD ROAD, SAN MARINO, CA 91108

At the Huntington you'll see it all: First editions of literary works, great works of art, beautiful gardens, wildlife (including several types of birds, squirrels, and koi fish in the ponds). In the Library, you'll find early editions of Shakespeare's works, Henry David Thoreau's manuscript of *Walden*, a Gutenberg Bible, and much more. The Art Collection includes 440 sculptures and 650 paintings with European art from the 15th to early 20th century and American art from the late 17th century to mid-20th century. Popular pieces include Thomas Gainsborough's *Blue Boy* and *Pinkie* by Sir Thomas Lawrence. 12 gardens with 15,000 different varieties of plants will give the kids lots to explore, including a rose garden, a California garden, a jungle garden, and more. And the Children's Garden gives kids the chance to learn about earth, air, fire, and water in an interactive, fun way. There's even an afternoon tea service.

# JET PROPULSION LABORATORY (JPL)

## 4800 OAK GROVE DR., PASADENA, CA 91109

If you've got a family member interested in outer space, then you must take advantage of the tours offered at Jet Propulsion Laboratory. Family tours (10 people or less) are offered; information about dates and reservations are available online. The tour begins with a presentation that explains the activities at JPL as well as visits to the Space Flight Operations Facility and the Spacecraft Assembly Facility.

This illustration combines an image of Jupiter from the JunoCam instrument aboard NASA's Juno spacecraft with a composite image of Earth to depict the size and depth of Jupiter's Great Red Spot.

CREDIT: JunoCam Image data: NASA/JPL-Caltech/SwRI/MSSSJunoCam Image processing by Kevin M. Gill (CC BY)Earth Image: NASA

## LOGAN'S CANDIES
### 125 W B STREET, ONTARIO, CA 91762

This old-fashioned candy shop has been in business since 1933, and they not only sell the good stuff, they make over 200 varieties of candy right in the shop! Aside from being able to buy delicious treats here, which is almost reason enough to visit, the added bonus is that you can actually watch them make the candy you are about to eat! This is an especially fun thing to do during the holiday season, as they are famous for their candy canes.

## LA COUNTY ARBORETUM
### 301 NORTH BALDWIN AVE, ARCADIA, CA 91007

Although you may be accosted by a peacock, it's worth it to visit this beautiful botanic garden just east of Los Angeles. The Los Angeles County Arboretum and Botanic Garden consists of 127 acres of plants, natural landscapes, wildlife and historic buildings. Families will view plants and trees from around the world at the

Aquatic Gardens, the Rainbow Serpent Garden, the Herb Garden, the Tropical Green House, and more. Historic structures on site include the Queen Anne Cottage, the Coach Barn, and the Reid-Baldwin Adobe. The Arboretum is also an official wildlife sanctuary. You'll see a variety of birds (including the famous peacocks), aquatic creatures, and small reptiles. The Arboretum also hosts a variety of special events throughout the year including festivals, movie screenings, musical performances, and holiday events.

## LOS ANGELES RIVER CENTER AND BIKE PATH

### 570 WEST AVENUE TWENTY-SIX, LOS ANGELES, CA 90065

The Los Angeles River runs through the City, and there are a number of places to get up close and explore, including at the Los Angeles River Center Bicycle Staging Area, where you'll find a self-service area complete with bike repair station, tire pump, bike racks, water fountain, restrooms, and picnic tables. There are multiple points of entry for the bike path; check the map online to determine the best route for your family. In the Summer, there are even spots along the river where you can kayak!

# MARCH FIELD AIR MUSEUM
## 22550 VAN BUREN BLVD., RIVERSIDE, CA 92518

Families can learn about the history of aviation when they visit the March Field Air Museum. You'll find one of the largest collections of military aircraft on the West Coast, including over 80 aircraft and more than 30,000 artifacts on display, some of which date back to World War I. Set on 30 acres of outdoor exhibit space, and with two indoor hangars as well, this museum is sure to keep you busy learning and exploring. On display is a full-scale replica aircraft from 1903 that helped launch the era of powered flight, as well as spy planes, unmanned aircraft, cargo planes, bombers, helicopters, and more.

# MARIACHI PLAZA

1817 E. 1st St., Los Angeles, CA 90033

Mariachi Plaza is named for the Mariachi musicians who gather at this spot waiting to be hired to play at community events, private parties, or in restaurants. The central gazebo you'll find at Mariachi Plaza was donated by Jalisco, Mexico, considered to be the birthplace of Mariachi music. Friday and Saturday nights the Plaza comes alive with food, music, and dancing. You'll also find the Boyle Hotel here (also referred to as the Mariachi Hotel), home to many of these Mariachi musicians.

# MOONLIGHT ROLLERWAY

5110 San Fernando Rd., Glendale, CA 91204

Once upon a time, this spot was a factory for airplane parts, but in 1956 it became a roller skating rink and families have enjoyed it ever since. If you already know how to skate, you're good to go, but they also offer lessons and have a pro shop with skates to rent or purchase. Terrific birthday party spot - oh, and you've probably seen it on TV or in the movies, since it's a popular place for Hollywood crews to film.

## MISSION INN MUSEUM
### 3696 MAIN ST., RIVERSIDE, CA 92501

The Mission Inn Museum features exhibits related to the history of the famous Mission Inn. Families can take a 75-minute tour which includes the Museum as well as parts of the Inn that the general public isn't usually able to see. The Mission Inn was first an adobe boarding house back in 1876; today it is an AAA four Diamond Historic site. The Museum's exhibits are related to the aviation and citrus industries, the California Missions, and they're well known for their annual Holiday Light displays.

## PALM SPRINGS

Palm Springs is a great destination for a family trip. There are beautiful spots for hiking, an aerial tramway kids of all ages love to ride, you can take a tour of the giant windmills, visit the Living Desert Zoo and Gardens, play tennis or golf, or just relax by the pool to beat the heat. And that's just scratching the surface.

## PLANES OF FAME AIR MUSEUM

14998 CAL AERO DR., CHINO, CA 91710

If your kids are into airplanes, the Planes of Fame Air Museum is a definite must-see! Located on the north side of the Chino Airport, Planes of Fame, which has a sister site in Arizona, is considered a living history museum because all the aircraft on display continue to fly. You can choose to explore by taking a self-guided tour or request a guided tour online. You'll be able to watch live flight demos of certain aircraft of select days, so be sure to check the website before you visit for an up-to-date aircraft flight and event schedule. Planes of Fame has an extensive collection of rare aircraft, and some have undergone detailed restoration in order to preserve the history they represent. With 5 hangars' worth of space, you're sure to see amazing aircraft at this unique spot.

# RAGING WATERS

## III RAGING WATERS DR., SAN DIMAS, CA 91773

Raging Waters is considered to be the largest water park in California. You'll find 50 acres of slides, rides, attractions, and a sand beach all set for family fun. Parents will feel comfortable knowing that young children have their own fun area including Kid's Kingdom and Splash Island.

# SAN GABRIEL MISSION

## 428 S. MISSION DRIVE SAN GABRIEL, CA 91776

Every 4th grader in California will learn the State's history, controversies and all, and when they get to the part about the Missions, some will even create the famous dioramas and models that are now sold as kits in some craft stores, carrying them precariously to school. Beat those 9-year-olds to the punch and visit the Mission you're probably closest to: San Gabriel.

## AMERICA'S TEACHING ZOO AT MOORPARK COLLEGE

## CHUMASH INDIAN MUSEUM

## GARDENS OF THE WORLD

## MARTIAL ARTS MUSEUM

## PICKWICK ICE AND PICKWICK BOWL

## REYES ADOBE HISTORICAL SITE

# The Valleys

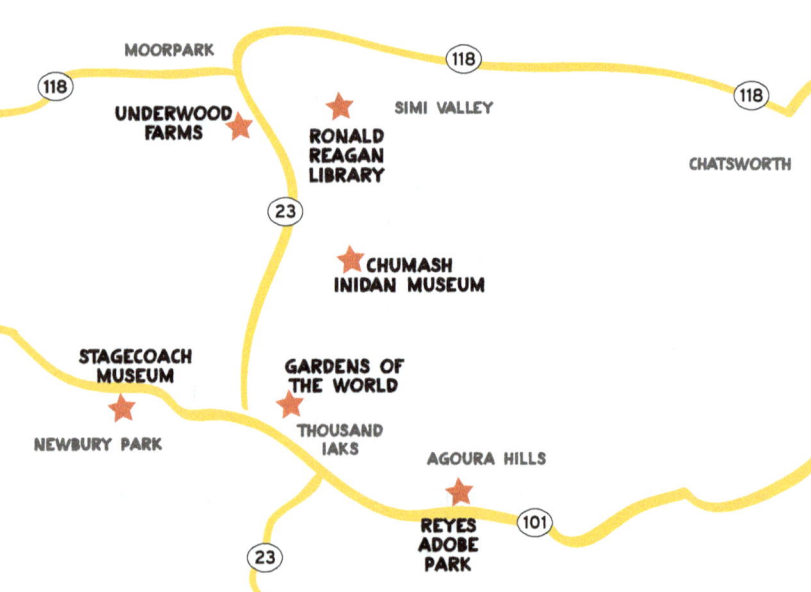

AMERICA'S TEACHING ZOO

MOORPARK

118

118

UNDERWOOD FARMS

SIMI VALLEY

118

RONALD REAGAN LIBRARY

CHATSWORTH

23

CHUMASH INIDAN MUSEUM

STAGECOACH MUSEUM

GARDENS OF THE WORLD

NEWBURY PARK

THOUSAND IAKS

AGOURA HILLS

REYES ADOBE PARK

101

23

# RONALD REAGAN LIBRARY
# AND PRESIDENTIAL MUSEUM
# STAGECOACH INN MUSEUM
# UNDERWOOD FAMILY FARMS
# WARNER BROS STUDIO TOUR
# WILDLIFE LEARNING CENTER
# WILLIAM S. HART MUSEUM

SANTA CLARITA

WILLIAM S. HART MUSEUM

NEWHALL

5

WILDLIFE
LEARNING
CENTER

210

SYLMAR

GRANADA
HILLS

118

5

210

NORTHRIDGE

405

5

170

MARTIAL ARTS MUSEUM

BURBANK

PICKWICK ICE

101

134

WARNER BROS.
STUDIO TOUR

GLENDALE

405

5

## AMERICA'S TEACHING ZOO AT MOORPARK COLLEGE

7075 CAMPUS RD., MOORPARK, CA 93021

America's Teaching Zoo is part of Moorpark College's Exotic animal Training and Management (EATM) Program which prepares students for careers in animal handling and training for the entertainment and wild-life education industries. There are often special animal presentations and training demonstrations, as well as special events throughout the year. This is a very small zoo and an easy one for young kids to experience.

## CHUMASH INDIAN MUSEUM

3290 LANG RANCH PARKWAY, THOUSAND OAKS, CA 91362

The Chumash Indian Museum serves as a living history center, giving families the chance to learn about the native Chumash Indians, one of the oldest tribes in the United States. You'll see a demonstration village, and there's a guided hike in the surrounding park.

# GARDENS OF THE WORLD
### 2001 THOUSAND OAKS BLVD., THOUSAND OAKS, CA 91362

Gardens of the World was founded by Mr. and Mrs. Hogan, the founders of "Pleasant Holidays." The Hogans wanted to share with others the beauty they found all around the world. As you stroll around the grounds, whether with a docent or on a self-guided tour, you'll encounter several themes, including a Japanese Garden, a Mission Courtyard, and an Italian Garden, among others.

# MARTIAL ARTS HISTORY MUSEUM
### 2319 W. MAGNOLIA BLVD., BURBANK, CA 91506

A visit to the Martial Arts History Museum provides families with the opportunity to learn about different Asian countries and the ways in which martial arts have influenced the traditions and history of these countries. In addition, families will learn about Martial Arts in America. The Museum also hosts a variety of special events throughout the year.

## PICKWICK ICE AND PICKWICK BOWL
### 921 AND 1001 RIVERSIDE DR., BURBANK, CA 91506

Escape the heat at Pickwick Ice, and try out your figure skating or hockey skills at this popular place, which features special hours each day for the public to come in and skate. They also host birthday parties and offer skating and hockey lessons. Nearby Pickwick Bowl offers twenty-four lanes of bowling fun. For kids, they have a fully automated bumper system and dragon ramps making bowling fun for all ages. There's also an on-site snack bar and pro shop.

## REYES ADOBE HISTORICAL SITE
### 30400 RAINBOW CREST DR., AGOURA HILLS, CA 91301

The Reyes Adobe was built in approximately 1850 and is considered to be Agoura Hills's first home. At this historic site, families will view different rooms of the home and get a sense of the way families used to live. You'll see artifacts, furnishings, documents, photos, and more on your docent-led tour.

# RONALD REAGAN PRESIDENTIAL LIBRARY AND MUSEUM

40 PRESIDENTIAL DR., SIMI VALLEY, CA 93065

The Ronald Reagan Presidential Library and Museum offers visitors the opportunity to learn about our country's 40th President. Exhibits include a look at Mr. Reagan's life – from his childhood, to his days as a GE spokesperson, to his acting days, and his time in politics – as the governor of California and then later as our nation's President. There's a full-size replica of the Oval Office (as it was decorated when Reagan was President, complete with jars of jelly beans), interactive opportunities like a classic field trip reenactment in the

Situation Room, but perhaps the most exciting thing is seeing Air Force One. The Air Force One on display is the same one that President Reagan (and six other Presidents) flew in. Families are able to step aboard, have a fun photo opportunity, view the cockpit, and walk the length of

this extraordinary plane! The Air Force One Pavilion also houses Marine One which families are welcome to step aboard as well (but watch your head!)

## STAGECOACH INN MUSEUM
### 51 S. VENTU PARK RD., NEWBURY PARK, CA 91320

You really get a sense of how times have changed when you explore the Stagecoach Inn Museum, which dates back to the 1800s. Over the years, this historic site served as a hotel, a post office, a restaurant, and a boys' military school. The Stagecoach Inn was named a California Landmark in 1965. Volunteer docents wear costumes from the period as they teach visitors about when the West was still Wild.

## UNDERWOOD FAMILY FARMS

### 3370 SUNSET VALLEY RD., MOORPARK, CA 93021

Underwood Family Farms is a terrific place for fun and to learn about life on a working farm. It's like someone combined a petting zoo with an amusement park. There are lots of activities to delight children, plenty of shade, and delicious fruits and vegetables as a bonus! They host many special events during the year, especially at Harvest and Holiday time, and you can even pick your own fruits and vegetables in season!

## WARNER BROS STUDIO TOUR

### 3400 WARNER BLVD., BURBANK, CA 91505

The Warner Bros. Studio Tour is a wonderful chance to peek behind the curtain and see how movies and TV shows are made, and visiting the Warner Bros. lot means you'll get a big dose of Hollywood history while you're at it. The tour begins with a movie overview of some of the classic films and TV shows that were filmed on the lot, and it makes for quite an impressive resume. Beginning with *The Jazz Singer* in 1927,

and continuing with films like *The Maltese Falcon*, *A Streetcar Named Desire*, *The Music Man*, *What's Up Doc*, *The Matrix* Trilogy and all the versions of *Ocean's Eleven*. Warner Bros. has been responsible for many great films – too many to name here. Plus, dozens and dozens of our favorite TV Shows come from Warner Bros., like *ER*, *Friends*, *Pretty Little Liars*, *Ellen*, *The West Wing*, *The Drew Carey Show*, and so many more. You'll also get access to exclusive dining options and the Studio Store for merch.

## WILDLIFE LEARNING CENTER

16027 YARNELL ST., SYLMAR, CA 91342

At the Wildlife Learning Center, families can learn about animals from around the world. There are more than 100 animals being cared for at this special facility. If you're looking for a more interactive experience you can choose an "Individual Animal Experience," such as feeding a porcupine, holding an owl, or meeting and touching a fennec fox. (These experiences require an additional fee.) Some of the animals here have been rescued, or were formerly inhabitants of Zoos, and they are all amazing.

## WILLIAM S. HART MUSEUM
### 24151 NEWHALL AVE., NEWHALL, CA 91321

Set on over 150 acres in Newhall, the William S. Hart Museum is a terrific place for families to visit, learn, and play. Once the home of the silent movie star for which it is named, the mansion and grounds are now a place where history comes alive: both the history of the movie industry in Southern California and the history of the American West. As a bonus, you'll be able to meet a small herd of Bison that live on the grounds, descendants of some that were once owned by Walt Disney, which is not something every museum can boast!

# MUSEUMS

DISCOVERY CUBE
LOS ANGELES

RONALD REAGAN
PRESIDENTIAL
MUSEUM

118

210

170

101

405

134

2

HUNTINGTON
LIBRARY ART
MUSEUM

KIDSPACE
CHILDREN'S
MUSEUM

SKIRBALL
CULTURAL
CENTER

ACADEMY
MUSEUM OF
MOTION
PICTURES

LA ZOO

AUTRY
MUSEUM

5

101

110

HERITAGE
SQUARE
MUSEUM

THE GETTY

LACMA

LA BREA
TAR PITS/PAGE
MUSEUM

CHINESE
AMERICAN
MUSEUM

10

GETTY
VILLA

PETERSON
AUTOMOTIVE
MUSEUM

GRAMMY
MUSEUM

JAPANESE
AMERICAN
MUSEUM

1

CAYTON
CHILDREN'S
MUSEUM

10

NAT. HISTORY
MUSEUM

CALIF. AFRICAN
AMERICAN
MUSEUM

5

MUSEUM
OF FLYING

CALIF. SCIENCE
CENTER

90

405

110

710

ZIMMERMAN
AUTOMOBILE
DRIVING MUSEUM

105

DISCOVERY CUBE
ORANGE COUNTY
(SANTA ANA)

WE
GOTTA
LOTTA
MUSEUMS!
YAY!

1

110

405

710

MUSEUM OF
LATIN
AMERICAN
ART

AQUARIUM
OF THE
PACIFIC

CABRILLO
MARINE
AQUARIUM

ACADEMY MUSEUM OF MOTION PICTURES
AQUARIUM OF THE PACIFIC
AUTRY MUSEUM
CABRILLO MARINE AQUARIUM
CALIFORNIA AFRICAN AMERICAN MUSEUM
CALIFORNIA SCIENCE CENTER
CAYTON CHILDREN'S MUSEUM
CHINESE AMERICAN MUSEUM
DISCOVERY CUBE LOS ANGELES AND ORANGE COUNTY
THE GETTY CENTER MUSEUM
THE GETTY VILLA
GRAMMY MUSEUM
HERITAGE SQUARE MUSEUM
HUNTINGTON LIBRARY, ART MUSEUM
AND BOTANICAL GARDENS
JAPANESE AMERICAN NATIONAL MUSEUM
KIDSEUM AT BOWERS MUSEUM
KIDSPACE CHILDREN'S MUSEUM
LA BREA TAR PITS AND PAGE MUSEUM
LA PLAZA DE CULTURA Y ARTES
LOS ANGELES COUNTY MUSEUM OF ART (LACMA)
LOS ANGELES FIRE DEPARTMENT MUSEUM
LOS ANGELES ZOO
LUCAS MUSEUM OF NARRATIVE ART
MARCH FIELD AIR MUSEUM
MUSEUM OF FLYING SANTA MONICA
MUSEUM OF LATIN AMERICAN ART
NATURAL HISTORY MUSEUM
PETERSEN AUTOMOTIVE MUSEUM
PRETEND CITY CHILDREN'S MUSEUM
RONALD REAGAN PRESIDENTIAL MUSEUM
SKIRBALL CULTURAL CENTER
USC PACIFIC ASIA MUSEUM
ZIMMERMAN AUTOMOBILE DRIVING MUSEUM

# AcAdemy museum of motion pictures

6067 Wilshire Blvd., Los AngeLes 90036

This is a fantastic place to take the whole family, especially if your family loves the movies. The core exhibition at the museum is called the Stories of Cinema, which offers celebratory, critical, and personal perspectives on cinema and the impact of movies on us all. You'll find costumes, props, script pages, and photographs from some of the most iconic and wonderful movies of all time. Some of the displays are quite imaginative and striking, like the Ruby Slippers worn by Dorothy from the Wizard of OZ set against a backdrop of the four travelers from the movie heading off across the

poppy fields to find the wizard. You'll also find displays of many of the mechanics of making films, like a motion picture camera on a dolly, and a film-editing machine, called a KEM, which has been all-but rendered useless by the use of video instead of film in movie making.

## AQUARIUM OF THE PACIFIC

(See Westside section)

# AUTRY MUSEUM

(See Hollywood section)

# CABRILLO MARINE AQUARIUM

(See Westside section)

# CALIFORNIA AFRICAN AMERICAN MUSEUM

600 STATE DR., LOS ANGELES, CA 90037

The California African American Museum, located within Exposition Park, focuses on the art and culture of African Americans, specifically focusing on California and the Western part of the United States. There are over 5000 objects in the permanent collection, ranging from the 1800s to the present, and includes painting, sculptures, works on paper, film, photographs, and historical documents.

# CALIFORNIA SCIENCE CENTER

(See Downtown section)

# CAYTON CHILDREN'S MUSEUM

395 SANTA MONICA PLACE MALL, SUITE 374, SANTA MONICA 90401

The Cayton Children's Museum is 21,000 square feet of discovery-based fun and hands-on exhibits that kids and adults will love. Formerly known as the Zimmer Children's Museum, the Cayton has moved to a new space, designed as five exhibit wings that are meant to inspire kids to explore, with lots of things they can touch and play with.

# CHINESE AMERICAN MUSEUM

425 N. Los Angeles St., Los Angeles, CA 90012

The Chinese American Museum is located at the El Pueblo de Los Angeles Historical Monument, inside one of the oldest surviving Chinese buildings in Southern California. Through the Museum's exhibits, visitors will learn about the role

Chinese-Americans have played throughout history. Different exhibits document different aspects of Chinese-American life.

## DISCOVERY CUBE LOS ANGELES AND ORANGE COUNTY

11800 FOOTHILL BLVD, SYLMAR, CA 91342 (L.A.)
2500 N MAIN STREET, SANTA ANA, CA 92805 (O.C.)

Southern California has two terrific, kid-friendly museums dedicated to hands-on science education, and your whole family can have fun at both Discovery Cube locations - Los Angeles and at the original Discovery Cube Orange County location in Santa Ana. The STEM and discovery activities each cater to young kids, with scavenger hunts, interactives, and many touchable exhibits. Spend time in the kid-sized Recycling plant, Grocery store, Physics stations, Wind/Climate Exhibits, and more.

## THE GETTY CENTER MUSEUM

1200 GETTY CENTER DR,
LOS ANGELES, CA 90049

The Getty is one of the most fun museums to visit with kids, even though neither the Getty Center nor the Getty Villa are technically Children's Museums per se. When you visit The Getty, you have the opportunity to view amazing art pieces as well as the opportunity to get a view of Los Angeles you don't often see. Children will most likely be intrigued before you even reach the Museum; riding the computer-operated trams from the parking lot is sure to get kids excited for what they're going to see at the top!

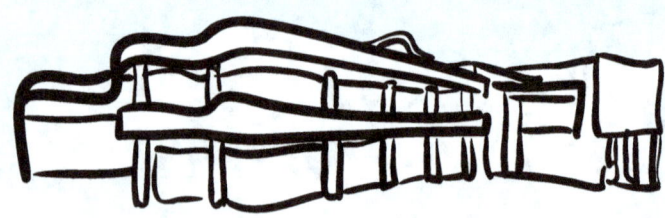

## THE GETTY VILLA
### 17985 PACIFIC COAST HIGHWAY, MALIBU, CA 90272

We love taking kids to the Getty Villa. There's a special exhibit made for kids to explore called the Family Forum, where it's OK to touch the reproductions of ancient pottery, and to play. The grounds are a beautiful place to stroll, and you'll see Greek and Roman antiquities, since the collection ranges from the Stone Age to the final days of the Roman Empire, including sculpture, jewelry, glassware, and more.

## GRAMMY MUSEUM

### 800 WEST OLYMPIC BLVD., LOS ANGELES, CA 90015

A trip to the GRAMMY Museum really isn't like any other museum visit. You'll see how the GRAMMY Award itself has evolved over time, becoming larger and larger. The Museum consists of four levels, and visitors are encouraged to start at the top and work their way down. You'll find costumes (an Elvis Presley shirt and Whitney Houston dress, for example), instruments, sheet music, and more behind glass cases. Headphones encourage visitors to stop and listen. There are also "mini-listening rooms" where families can learn about the evolution of pop music, for example, or hear how the quality of music listening has changed from the very earliest phonographs to cassettes to compact discs to iPods.

# HERITAGE SQUARE MUSEUM
3800 HOMER STREET, LOS ANGELES, CA 90031

Heritage Square is made up of eight beautiful buildings, constructed in the Victorian Era, and preserved in order to demonstrate what life was like in the early days of Los Angeles. There are Living History performances and special events like Museums of the Arroyo Day, and special holiday events each year as well.

# HUNTINGTON LIBRARY, ART MUSEUM AND BOTANICAL GARDENS

(See Points East section)

# JAPANESE AMERICAN NATIONAL MUSEUM
100 N. CENTRAL AVE., LOS ANGELES, CA 90012

The Japanese American National Museum is a one-of-a-kind place, dedicated to the history of Japanese Americans, and to a deeper understanding of cultural diversity. There are frank depictions of the discrimination many Japanese

Americans faced during World War II, along with educational resources for children. The Museum celebrates the cultural contributions made by Japanese Americans and hosts many special events throughout the year, each designed to be welcoming and educational.

## KIDSEUM AT BOWERS MUSEUM
1802 N. MAIN ST., SANTA ANA, CA 92706

*NOTE:* At the time of publication, Kidseum is undergoing renovations, and we hope they'll have re-opened by the time you read this. Family programming continues at the Bowers Museum. Kidseum gives kids the opportunity to learn about cultures and art from around the world. Kids will find many ways to be actively engaged here including creating art, being an archaeologist for a day, traveling through time (through the magic of the Green Screen Time Machine), and more.

## KIDSPACE CHILDREN'S MUSEUM
480 N. ARROYO BLVD., PASADENA, CA 91103

Kidspace Children's Museum has everything you need for a fun day out with kids including interactive exhibits, lots of places to run around and plenty of things to do and see. Kidspace was designed for kids ages 1-10, and is a place families could

easily spend all day. There are several "zones," and each has terrific learn and play opportunities. The Arroyo Adventure is filled with interactive exhibits, like the Hawk's Nest, the Flood and Erosion Plain, Mud and Clay play, and others. Kids can splash in the simulated river as well, so bringing a change of clothes is not a bad idea.

## LA BREA TAR PITS AND PAGE MUSEUM
### 5801 WILSHIRE BLVD, LOS ANGELES, CA 90036

The La Brea Tar Pits and Page Museum is one of the coolest places to visit in Los Angeles. Not only can you

see the world's largest collection of Ice Age Fossils on display, you can get up close to bubbling tar (do your best not to step in it). As you wander through the La Brea Tar Pits and Page Museum, you may feel as if you're walking back in time. You'll see fossils from at least 650 different species, including  dire wolves, ancient horses, the Columbian mammoth, coyotes, and more. You'll learn just how animals could become trapped in just a few inches of tar. And you can even watch paleontologists at work right in front of your eyes through the glass walls of the Fossil Lab.

## LA PLAZA DE CULTURA Y ARTES
### 501 N MAIN ST., LOS ANGELES 90012

A visit to this museum will illuminate the role played by Mexicans, Mexican Americans, and Latinos in helping to create the Los Angeles we live in. Through exhibitions about the history of Los Angeles, as well as galleries filled with art, this museum is meant to be enjoyed by all. There's also a beautiful garden and event space outside, and they host

family programming throughout the year. As a bonus, their location near Olvera Street, Union Station, and the Chinese American Museum means you can make it a full day of LA History.

## LOS ANGELES COUNTY MUSEUM OF ART (LACMA)

5905 WILSHIRE BLVD., Los Angeles, CA 90036

LACMA is a cool art museum and sculpture garden, and with a NexGenLA membership, you can take your kids there all the time. The membership is for LA County kids 17 and younger, and offers free admission to the permanent collection, and each child gets to bring 1 accompanying adult with them, also for free. Outside, on the grounds, you'll find the iconic Lightpole sculpture every aspiring instagrammer needs to be photographed near, as well as Levitated Mass, a giant boulder positioned above a walkway kids (and adults) love to see.

## LOS ANGELES FIRE DEPARTMENT MUSEUM

### 1335 N. CAHUENGA BLVD., HOLLYWOOD, CA 90028

Kids who love learning about firefighters will love visiting the L.A. Fire Department Museum in Hollywood. Families will view classic LAFD vehicles and equipment, memorabilia, and there's also a special kids education center. The Museum is housed in Old Fire Station 27. Check their website for up-to-date hours and programming.

## LOS ANGELES ZOO

(See Hollywood section)

## LUCAS MUSEUM OF NARRATIVE ART

### EXPOSITION PARK, LOS ANGELES 90007

Under construction at the time of publication, this is sure to be one of the most highly anticipated museum openings anywhere. Founded by filmmaker George Lucas and his wife Mellody Hobson, the

museum will be dedicated to the art of visual storytelling. The building is sure to transform Exposition Park, with a purported 100,000 square feet of gallery space and 11 acres of surrounding green space. We can't wait!

# MARCH FIELD

(See Points East section)

# MUSEUM OF FLYING SANTA MONICA
## 3100 AIRPORT AVE., SANTA MONICA, CA 90405

For aviation enthusiasts, a visit to the Museum of Flying is a must-do. Families will find artifacts from the Douglas Aircraft Company, aviation-related art, a replica of the Wright Flyer, a flight simulator, and more. There is also an interactive center for children. And you  can sit in the pilot's chair of a FedEx plane, positioned at the actual height.

# MUSEUM OF LATIN AMERICAN ART
## 628 ALAMITOS AVENUE, LONG BEACH, CA 90802

The Museum of Latin American Art is the only museum within the United States that is dedicated to both modern and contemporary Latin American art. Families will enjoy their permanent collection which includes more than 1,300 works of art, including sculpture, painting,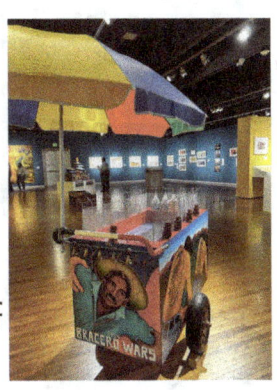

photography, and video, all created by more than 350 Latin American artists from 20 Latin American countries. There are special events held throughout the year, all worth checking out.

## NATURAL HISTORY MUSEUM
(See Downtown section)

## PETERSEN AUTOMOTIVE MUSEUM
6060 WILSHIRE BLVD., Los Angeles, CA 90036

The Petersen Automotive Museum has over 25 exhibits showcasing more than 300 cars, including famous Hollywood cars, vintage cars, Hot Rods, and Pixar Cars. The Museum's design includes three floors (the History floor, the Industry floor, and the Artistry floor). Perfect for kids is the Cars-themed Mechanical Institute Discovery Center — a fully interactive experience.

# PRETEND CITY CHILDREN'S MUSEUM
## 29 HUBBLE, IRVINE, CA 92618

At Pretend City, kids have the chance to be actively engaged and learn how the real world works. Pretend City describes itself as "the world in a nutshell." 17 interactive exhibits and activities allow kids to

practice problem solving, critical thinking, math skills, and more. Exhibits include an art studio, a cafe, a post office, a grocery store, and more. The Museum is a nut-free facility.

# RONALD REAGAN PRESIDENTIAL MUSEUM

(See Valleys section)

# SKIRBALL CULTURAL CENTER
## 2701 N. SEPULVEDA BLVD., Los Angeles, CA 90049

In addition to its permanent exhibits, the Skirball hosts a variety of special events throughout the year, including sing-alongs, musical performances, and film screenings. Special family-friendly high-

lights include the Family Art Studio (where children and their parents can create their own art projects), and Noah's Ark. In this special place, children can build, climb, explore, and play while marveling at the floor-to-ceiling wooden ark filled with unique animals.

## USC PACIFIC ASIA MUSEUM
### 46 NORTH LOS ROBLES AVE., PASADENA 91101

Located in an historic building designed to resemble an Imperial Chinese Palace, this is a fun museum to visit. You'll see artifacts from many different Asian cultures, displayed in a beautiful setting. There's an interactive gallery called Exploring the Silk Road, which is part of the permanent collection, and it's ideal for families. You'll find a spot to sit and read, musical instruments kids can touch, a Camel kids can sit upon, and more. And kids are sure to love seeing the koi fish in the garden pond.

# ZIMMERMAN AUTOMOBILE DRIVING MUSEUM

## 610 LAIRPORT ST., EL SEGUNDO, CA 90245

Families who are interested in cars should definitely make a point to visit the Automobile Driving Museum. You'll find over 100 vintage and antique automobiles out on display. The Museum's purpose is to preserve automotive history and to educate the public. In addition, kids will have fun with a scavenger hunt, playing in a special area with cars and Legos, as well as climbing into two cars on display.

# THEME PARKS

MAGIC MOUNTAIN

5

210

118

210

BURBANK

101

134

UNIVERSAL STUDIOS

405

10

DOWNTOWN L.A.

SANTA MONICA

10

5

605

110

91

605

KNOTT'S BERRY FARM

TORRANCE

405

ADVENTURE CITY

LONG BEACH

5

57

DISNEYLAND

39

GREAT WOLF LODGE

SANTA ANA

405

5

HUNTINGTON BEACH

10

60

215

FIESTA FAMILY FUN VILLAGE

15

91

15

215

210

210

15

10

10

10

60

60

71

RIVERSIDE

15

91

CASTLE PARK

57

91

CORONA

ADVENTURE CITY

CASTLE PARK

DISNEYLAND AND
DISNEY CALIFORNIA ADVENTURE

FIESTA VILLAGE
FAMILY FUN PARK

KNOTT'S BERRY FARM

GREAT WOLF LODGE

SIX FLAGS MAGIC MOUNTAIN

UNIVERSAL STUDIOS HOLLYWOOD

# ADVENTURE CITY

1238 S BEACH BLVD, ANAHEIM, CA 92804

Adventure City is an amusement park designed for families with young kids. The rides are not too fast or scary, the park is not too big, and the prices are not too high. There's a train ride, a petting zoo, a carousel, there are interactive shows, and you can even book a birthday party here.

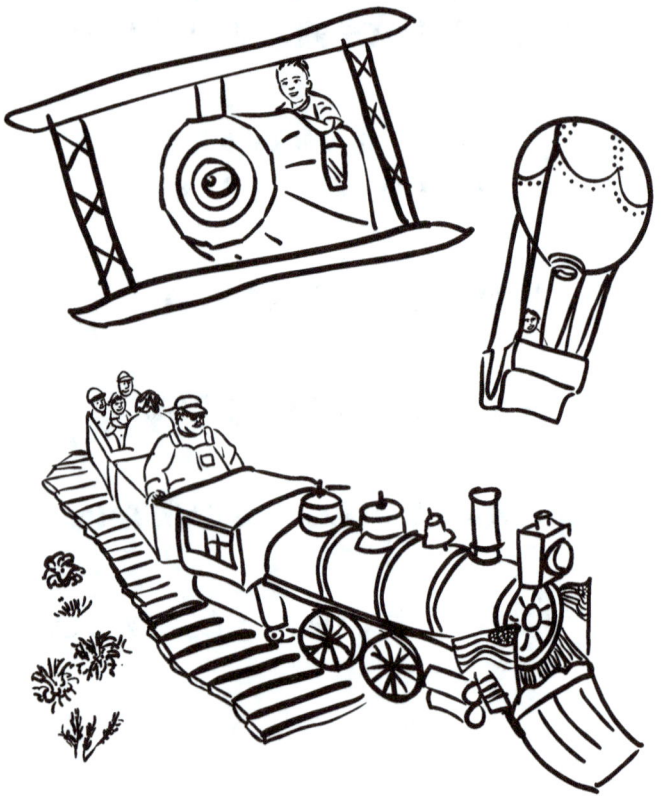

# CASTLE PARK

3500 POLK ST., RIVERSIDE, CA 92505

(See Points East section)

# DISNEYLAND AND DISNEY CALIFORNIA ADVENTURE

1313 HARBOR BLVD., ANAHEIM, 92803

Disneyland opened in 1955, and has aimed to be the "Happiest Place on Earth" ever since. The home of Mickey Mouse has expanded and been refreshed and reinvented over the years, keeping up with their ever-expanding Universe of characters and themes, and it's still setting the gold standard for theme parks. Disney California Adventure opened up right next door in 2001, and offers an entirely new park experience, separate from Disneyland. Each have their charms, must-do experiences, and fan-favorite dining spots, so it's worth considering finding the time to play at both.

## FIESTA VILLAGE FAMILY FUN PARK

(See Points East section)

## KNOTT'S BERRY FARM

### 8039 BEACH BLVD, BUENA PARK, CA 90620

Founded in 1920, Knott's Berry Farm began as an actual berry farm, and over the years turned into the amusement park we know today. There are rides and games, and an Old West Ghost Town feel to the park, which is also known for their jellies and Mrs. Knott's Fried Chicken - a dining experience you must try. Snoopy and the Peanuts Gang hang out at Knott's, and look for special events at Halloween and Christmas every year. And each Summer you can enjoy Knott's Soak City Water Park!

## GREAT WOLF LODGE

### 12681 HARBOR BOULEVARD, GARDEN GROVE CA 92840

Great Wolf Lodge hotels have indoor water parks and activities designed to keep kids entertained and families happy - and they offer Day Passes as well! The Northern Lights Arcade is like a tiny Vegas for kids - games yield tickets, which can be traded in for prizes. There's also  Howl at the Moon Glow Golf (mini golf with black lights), and they have a unique interactive game called MagiQuest, that takes you on a magical scavenger hunt throughout the hotel.

## SIX FLAGS MAGIC MOUNTAIN

### 26101 MAGIC MOUNTAIN PKWY, VALENCIA, CA 91355

They don't call this place the Thrill Capital of the World for nothing. Six Flags Magic Mountain is THE place to go for roller coaster riding in Southern California. This theme park sits on 250+ acres and has over 100 rides and attractions. They have helpfully categorized things for us into Thrill Rides, Family Rides, and Kids Rides, so we can easily know what to get in line for depending on our appetite for speed and twists and turns. Or not so much. There are also live shows and experiences at Magic Mountain. Here you'll see characters from the DC Comics Universe, like the Justice League, as well as cartoon favorites from the Looney Tunes catalog, like Bugs Bunny and Daffy Duck. Whether they're singing and dancing, enacting a mock battle, or just hanging out for a Meet and Greet, you're sure to have fun with them.

## UNIVERSAL STUDIOS HOLLYWOOD

### 100 UNIVERSAL CITY PLAZA, UNIVERSAL CITY, CA 91608

Universal Studios is a theme park set on an actual movie studio lot, and they're famous for the Tram Tour with behind the scenes tidbits about classic Universal Studios movies and TV shows. Over the years, they've expanded the experiences at the park, and now visitors will find rides like Jurassic World, the Mummy, and Transformers, as well as the delightful Wizarding World of Harry Potter. You'll feel like you're in a snow-capped town of Hogsmeade, complete with Honeydukes, the candy shop from the books, Ollivander's wand shop, and of course a couple of gift shops. Universal CityWalk is right next door, with multiple places to shop and dine.

"From the South Bay to the Valley
From the West Side to the East Side
Everybody's very happy
'Cause the sun is shining all the time
Looks like another perfect day
I love L.A. (we love it)
I love L.A. (we love it)
We love it!"

- Randy Newman, "I Love LA"

# FUN IDEAS FOR THINGS TO DO WITH TODDLERS!

- Carousel at Santa Monica Pier
- Beach Time all along the coast
- Aquarium of the Pacific
- Park Time at one of the many, many parks in SoCal
- Annenberg Community Beach House
- Discovery Cube
- Pretend City
- Kidspace Children's Museum
- Cayton Museum
- Petersen Museum
- Huntington Library and Museum Children's Garden
- Descanso Gardens
- Griffith Park Pony Rides
- Getty Center Museum
- Underwood Family Farm

# Awesome ideas for things to do with teens!

- Rock Climbing at an indoor gym
- Parasailing, Kayaking, or stand-up Paddleboarding
- Horseback Riding
- Roller Skating at Moonlight Rollerway
- iFly Indoor Skydiving
- Escape Rooms
- Indoor Kart Racing
- Ride the LA River Bike Path
- Summer Educational Programs
- Six Flags Magic Mountain, Universal Studios Hollywood, Disneyland
- Family Hikes
- Visit Local Colleges

# IDEAS FOR SEASONAL FUN
# + ANNUAL EVENTS AND FESTIVALS

### JANUARY

- Tournament of Roses Parade (always held on New Year's Day)
- Festival of Human Abilities at Aquarium
- Martin Luther King Day Celebration at CAAM
- Oshogatsu Family festival at JANM
- Whale Fiesta at Cabrillo Marine Aquarium
- Head to the SoCal mountains to play in the snow

### FEBRUARY

- African American History Festivals at Aquarium of the Pacific, CAAM and other spots
- Lunar New Year Festivals in Chinatown and other spots
- Valentine's Day Events

### MARCH

- International Children's Festival at Aquarium
- LA Nature Fest at Natural History Museum + opening of the Butterfly Pavilion
- Grunion Fishtival at Cabrillo Marine Aquarium
- LA Marathon
- Passover Celebrations (unless Passover occurs in April of that year)
- Blessing of the Animals at Olvera Street (Sunday before Easter)
- Conejo Valley Days

## APRIL

- See Spring Wildflowers in Bloom
- LA Times Festival of Books
- Easter Celebrations (unless Easter occurs in March of that year)
- California Poppy Festival
- Skirball Puppet Festival
- Santa Clarita Cowboy Festival
- Original Renaissance Pleasure Faire
- Acura Grand Prix of Long Beach

## MAY

- LA County Fair (new dates beginning in 2022)
- Fiesta Broadway
- Cinco de Mayo Festival Olvera Street
- Fiesta Hermosa
- Go Strawberry-Picking
- Great Big Family Play Day
- Celebrate Mother's Day

## JUNE

- Celebrate Juneteenth
- Pacific Islander Festival
- Pride Festival West Hollywood
- Pasadena Chalk Festival
- Go Cherry-Picking
- Leona Valley Cherry Parade and Festival
- Celebrate Father's Day
- Numerous Outdoor activities take place in Summer, like concerts and movies

- Many local Public pools and Water Parks open to keep us cool

**JULY**
- 4th of July Parades, Block Parties, and Fireworks
- Lotus Festival
- Long Beach Dragon Boat Festival
- Festival of Arts and Pageant of the Masters
- Blueberry-picking
- Cool off at a Water Park

**AUGUST**
- Fiesta La Ballona
- LA Taco Festival
- Nisei Week Japanese Festival Little Tokyo
- Go Camping
- CicLAvia - open streets event takes place 3-4 times per year in different parts of Los Angeles)

**SEPTEMBER**
- Dino Fest at Natural History Museum + Spider Pavilion opens
- Fiesta Hermosa 2nd time
- Moopetam Native American Festival
- Abbot Kinney Festival
- Annual Watts Tower Day of the Drum and Jazz Festival

**OCTOBER**
- Numerous Halloween and Harvest Festivals
- Underwood Family Farms
- Mr. Bones Pumpkin Patch

- Nights of the Jack
- Carved at Descanso
- Go Apple-Picking

## NOVEMBER
- Numerous Día de Los Muertos celebrations
- Hollywood Forever Cemetery
- Forest Lawn Cemetery
- Olvera Street
- Autumn Festival at Aquarium
- Volunteer to Help Serve Thanksgiving Dinner to Those in Need
- Hollywood Christmas Parade (Sunday after Thanksgiving)

## DECEMBER
- Numerous Hanukkah Festivals and Events (unless Hanukkah occurs in November that year)
- Numerous Christmas Festivals and Events
- Hanukkah at the Skirball
- Enchanted Forest of Light at Descanso
- Candy Cane Lane neighborhood events, like El Segundo and Altadena
- Christmas on the Farm at Underwood
- Mission Inn Museum Riverside annual light show
- LA County Holiday Celebration at Dorothy Chandler/ Music Center
- Marina del Rey Holiday Boat Parade
- Las Posadas (Olvera Street)
- Celebrate New Year's Eve
- Head back to the mountains for snow play

# APPENDIX

## DOWNTOWN

**Angels Flight Railway**
Top Entrance: California Plaza, 350 South Grand Avenue, Los Angeles 90071
The Lower Entrance: 351 South Hill Street, Los Angeles 90013
https://www.angelsflight.org/

**Bradbury Building**
304 S. Broadway, Los Angeles, CA 90013
https://www.laconservancy.org/locations/bradbury-building

**California Science Center**
700 Exposition Park Dr, Los Angeles, CA 90037
https://californiasciencecenter.org/

**Central Library**
630 W. 5th Street, Los Angeles, CA 90071
https://www.lapl.org/branches/central-library

**City Hall**
200 N. Spring Street, Los Angeles, CA 90012
https://www.lacity.org/

**Fashion District**
Multiple Blocks around Santee and Olympic in DTLA
https://fashiondistrict.org/

**Grand Central Market**
317 S Broadway, Los Angeles, CA 90013
https://www.grandcentralmarket.com/

**Grand Park and Fountain**
200 N Grand Ave, Los Angeles, CA 90012
https://grandparkla.org/

**Little Tokyo**
Los Angeles 90012
https://www.golittletokyo.com/

**Natural History Museum**
900 W Exposition Blvd, Los Angeles, CA 90007
https://nhm.org/

**Olvera Street**
Los Angeles, CA 90012
https://elpueblo.lacity.org/

**LA Live**
800 West Olympic Blvd., Los Angeles 90015
https://www.lalive.com/
800 W. Olympic Blvd. / Los Angeles, California 90015

**The Last Bookstore**
453 South Spring Street, Los Angeles, CA 90013
https://www.lastbookstorela.com/

**Union Station**
800 N Alameda St, Los Angeles, CA 90012
https://www.unionstationla.com/

**Walt Disney Concert Hall**
111 S Grand Ave, Los Angeles, CA 90012
https://www.laphil.com/

**Watts Towers**
1727 E 107th St, Los Angeles, CA 90002
https://www.wattstowers.org/

## HOLLYWOOD + GRIFFITH PARK

**Autry Museum of the American West**
4700 Western Heritage Way, Los Angeles, CA 90027
https://theautry.org/

**El Capitan Theater**
6838 Hollywood Blvd., Los Angeles, CA 90028
https://elcapitantheatre.com/

**Fern Dell Hike, Griffith Park**
Fern Dell Dr, Los Angeles, CA 90027
https://www.laparks.org/griffithpark/

**Griffith Observatory**
2800 E. Observatory Rd., Los Angeles, CA 90027
https://griffithobservatory.org/

**Griffith Park Pony Rides**
4400 Crystal Springs Dr., Los Angeles, CA 90027
https://www.griffithparkponyride.com/

**Guinness World Records Museum**
6764 Hollywood Blvd., Hollywood, CA 90028
https://www.guinnessmuseumhollywood.com/

**Hollywood Bowl**
2301 N Highland Ave, Los Angeles, CA 90068
https://www.hollywoodbowl.com/

**Hollywood Forever Cemetery**
6000 Santa Monica Blvd., Los Angeles, CA 90038
https://hollywoodforever.com/

**Hollywood Museum**
1660 N. Highland Ave., Hollywood, CA 90028
https://www.thehollywoodmuseum.com/

**Hollywood Sign**
Los Angeles, CA 90068
https://hollywoodsign.org/

**Hollywood Walk of Fame**
Hollywood Blvd between La Brea and Gower and on Vine Street from Sunset to Yucca 90028
https://walkoffame.com/

**Hollywood Wax Museum**
6767 Hollywood Blvd., Los Angeles, CA 90028
https://www.hollywoodwaxentertainment.com/hollywood-ca-attractions/

**Los Angeles Zoo**
5333 Zoo Drive, Los Angeles, CA 90027
https://www.lazoo.org/

**Ripley's Believe it or Not Odditorium**
6780 Hollywood Blvd., Hollywood 90028
https://www.ripleys.com/

**Travel Town Museum**
5200 Zoo Drive, Griffith Park, Los Angeles, CA 90027
https://traveltown.org/

# WESTSIDE (AND ALONG THE COAST)

**The Adamson House and Malibu Museum**
23200 Pacific Coast Highway, Malibu, CA 90265
https://www.parks.ca.gov/?page_id=672

**Annenberg Community Beach House**
415 Pacific Coast Highway, Santa Monica, CA 90402
https://www.annenbergbeachhouse.com/

**Aquarium of the Pacific**
100 Aquarium Way, Long Beach, CA 90802
https://www.aquariumofpacific.org/

**Baldwin Hills Scenic Overlook**
6300 Hetzler Rd., Culver City, CA 90232
https://www.parks.ca.gov/?page_id=22790

**Battleship IOWA in San Pedro**
250 S. Harbor Blvd., San Pedro, CA 90731
https://www.pacificbattleship.com/

**Rodeo Drive in Beverly Hills**
Between Wilshire Blvd and Santa Monica Blvd., Beverly Hills 90212
https://rodeodrive-bh.com/

**Cabrillo Marine Aquarium**
3720 Stephen M. White Dr., San Pedro, CA 90731
https://www.cabrillomarineaquarium.org/

**Catalina Island**
Catalina, CA 90704
https://www.visitcatalinaisland.com/

**Douglas Park Santa Monica**
2439 Wilshire Blvd., Santa Monica, CA
https://www.smgov.net/Departments/CCS/content.aspx?id=31694

**Korean Bell of Friendship**
Angels Gate Park
3601 S. Gaffey St., San Pedro, CA 90731
https://sanpedro.com/san-pedro-area-points-interest/korean-bell-friendship/

**Malibu Beach - Point Dume**
7103 Westward Beach Road, Malibu, CA 90265
https://beaches.lacounty.gov/point-dume-beach/

### Malibu Creek State Park
1925 Las Virgenes Road, Calabasas, CA 91302
https://www.parks.ca.gov/?page_id=614

### Mother's Beach
4101 Admiralty Way, Marina del Rey, CA 90292
https://beaches.lacounty.gov/marina-beach/

### Palisades Park and Camera Obscura
Adjacent to Ocean Avenue, between Colorado Avenue and Adelaide Drive
https://www.smgov.net/Departments/CCS/content.aspx?id=31700

### Santa Monica Pier
200 Santa Monica Pier, Santa Monica 90401
At the very end of Colorado Blvd and the Pacific Ocean
https://www.santamonicapier.org/

### STAR Eco Station
10101 Jefferson Blvd., Culver City, CA 90232
https://www.ecostation.org/

### Temescal Gateway Canyon Hike
15601 Sunset Blvd., Pacific Palisades, CA
https://mrca.ca.gov/parks/park-listing/temescal-gateway-park/

### Theatricum Botanicum
1419 N. Topanga Canyon Blvd., Topanga, CA 90290
https://theatricum.com/

### Tongva Park
1615 Ocean Ave., Santa Monica, CA 90401
https://tongvapark.smgov.net/

### Topanga Canyon Horseback Riding
2623 Old Topanga Canyon Road, Topanga, CA 90290
https://www.losangeleshorsebackriding.com/

### UCLA Campus
Westwood, Los Angeles 90095
https://www.ucla.edu/

### Venice Beach and Boardwalk, Venice Canals, and Venice Skate Park
1800 Ocean Front Walk, Los Angeles 90291
https://www.laparks.org/venice/

**Will Rogers State Park**
1501 Will Rogers Park Rd., Pacific Palisades, CA 90272
https://www.parks.ca.gov/?page_id=626


## POINTS EAST

**Castle Park**
3500 Polk St., Riverside, CA 92505
https://www.castlepark.com/en

**Descanso Gardens**
1418 Descanso Drive, La Cañada Flintridge, CA 91011
https://www.descansogardens.org/

**Frank G. Bonelli Park**
120 Via Verde Park Rd., San Dimas, CA 91773
https://parks.lacounty.gov/frank-g-bonelli-regional-park/

**Fiesta Village Family Fun Park**
1405 E Washington St, Colton, CA 92324
https://www.fiestavillage.com/

**Huntington Library, Art Museum and Botanical Gardens**
1151 Oxford Road, San Marino, CA 91108
https://www.huntington.org/

**Jet Propulsion Laboratory (JPL)**
4800 Oak Grove Dr., Pasadena, CA 91109
https://www.jpl.nasa.gov/events/tours/views/

**Logan's Candies**
125 W B Street, Ontario, CA 91762
https://www.facebook.com/loganscandies/

**LA County Arboretum**
301 North Baldwin Ave, Arcadia, CA 91007
https://www.arboretum.org/

**Los Angeles River Center and Bike Path**
570 West Avenue Twenty-Six, Los Angeles, CA 90065
https://mrca.ca.gov/wedding-special-events/pages/los-angeles-river-center-gar-dens/

**March Field Air Museum**
22550 Van Buren Blvd., Riverside, CA 92518
https://www.marchfield.org/

**Mariachi Plaza**
1817 E. 1st St., Los Angeles, CA 90033
https://mariachiplazalosangeles.com/site/

**Moonlight Rollerway**
5110 San Fernando Rd., Glendale, CA 91204
https://moonlightrollerway.com/

**Mission Inn Museum**
3696 Main St., Riverside, CA 92501
https://missioninnmuseum.org/

**Palm Springs**
https://visitpalmsprings.com/

**Planes of Fame Air Museum**
14998 Cal Aero Dr., Chino, CA 91710
https://planesoffame.org/

**Raging Waters**
111 Raging Waters Dr., San Dimas, CA 91773
https://www.ragingwaters.com/

**San Gabriel Mission**
428 S. Mission Drive San Gabriel, CA 91776
https://www.sangabrielmissionchurch.org/

## THE VALLEYS

**America's Teaching Zoo at Moorpark College**
7075 Campus Rd., Moorpark, CA 93021
https://zoo.moorparkcollege.edu

**Chumash Indian Museum**
3290 Lang Ranch Parkway, Thousand Oaks, CA 91362
https://www.chumashmuseum.org/

**Gardens of the World**
2001 Thousand Oaks Blvd., Thousand Oaks, CA 91362
http://www.gardensoftheworld.info/

**Martial Arts History Museum**
2319 W. Magnolia Blvd., Burbank, CA 91506
https://martialartsmuseum.com/

**Pickwick Ice and Pickwick Bowl**
921 and 1001 Riverside Dr., Burbank, CA 91506
https://www.lakingsicepickwick.com/
https://www.pickwickbowl.com/

**Reyes Adobe Historical Site**
30400 Rainbow Crest Dr., Agoura Hills, CA 91301
https://conejo.com/?to_do=reyes-adobe-historical-site-2

**Ronald Reagan Presidential Library and Museum**
40 Presidential Dr., Simi Valley, CA 93065
https://www.reaganfoundation.org/library-museum/

**Stagecoach Inn Museum**
51 S. Ventu Park Rd., Newbury Park, CA 91320
https://stagecoachinnmuseum.com/

**Underwood Family Farms**
3370 Sunset Valley Rd., Moorpark, CA 93021
https://www.underwoodfamilyfarms.com/

**Warner Bros Studio Tour**
3400 Warner Blvd., Burbank, CA 91505
https://www.wbstudiotour.com/tour/studio/

**Wildlife Learning Center**
16027 Yarnell St., Sylmar, CA 91342
https://wildlifelearningcenter.org/

**William S. Hart Museum**
24151 Newhall Ave., Newhall, CA 91321
https://hartmuseum.org/

## MUSEUMS

**Academy Museum of Motion Pictures**
6067 Wilshire Blvd., Los Angeles 90036
https://www.academymuseum.org/en/

**Aquarium of the Pacific**
100 Aquarium Way, Long Beach, CA 90802
https://www.aquariumofpacific.org/

**Automobile Driving Museum**
610 Lairport St., El Segundo, CA 90245
https://www.automobiledrivingmuseum.org/

**Autry Museum**
4700 Western Heritage Way, Los Angeles, CA 90027
https://theautry.org/

**Cabrillo Marine Aquarium**
3720 Stephen M. White Dr., San Pedro, CA 90731
https://www.cabrillomarineaquarium.org/

**California African American Museum**
600 State Dr., Los Angeles, CA 90037
https://www.caamuseum.org/

**California Science Center**
700 Exposition Park Dr, Los Angeles, CA 90037
https://californiasciencecenter.org/

**Cayton Children's Museum**
395 Santa Monica Place Mall, Suite 374, Santa Monica 90401
https://www.caytonmuseum.org/

**Chinese American Museum**
425 N. Los Angeles St., Los Angeles, CA 90012
https://camla.org/

**Discovery Cube Los Angeles and Orange County**
11800 Foothill Blvd, Sylmar, CA 91342
2500 N Main Street, Santa Ana, CA 92805
https://www.discoverycube.org/

**GRAMMY Museum**
800 West Olympic Blvd., Los Angeles, CA 90015
https://grammymuseum.org/

**The Getty Center**
1200 Getty Center Dr, Los Angeles, CA 90049
https://www.getty.edu/

**The Getty Villa**
17985 Pacific Coast Highway, Malibu, CA 90272
https://www.getty.edu/

**Heritage Square Museum**
3800 Homer Street, Los Angeles, CA 90031
http://heritagesquare.org/

**Huntington Library, Art Museum and Botanical Gardens**
1151 Oxford Road, San Marino, CA 91108
https://www.huntington.org/

**Japanese American National Museum**
100 N. Central Ave., Los Angeles, CA 90012
https://www.janm.org/

**Kidseum at Bowers Museum**
1802 N. Main St., Santa Ana, CA 92706
https://www.bowers.org/

**Kidspace Children's Museum**
480 N. Arroyo Blvd., Pasadena, CA 91103
https://kidspacemuseum.org/

**La Brea Tar Pits and Page Museum**
5801 Wilshire Blvd, Los Angeles, CA 90036
https://tarpits.org/

**La Plaza de Cultura y Artes**
501 N Main St., Los Angeles 90012
https://lapca.org/

**Los Angeles County Museum of Art (LACMA)**
5905 Wilshire Blvd., Los Angeles, CA 90036
https://www.lacma.org/

**Los Angeles Fire Department Museum**
1335 N. Cahuenga Blvd., Hollywood, CA 90028
https://www.lafdmuseum.org/

**Los Angeles Zoo and Botanical Gardens**
5333 Zoo Drive, Los Angeles, CA 90027
https://www.lazoo.org/

**Lucas Museum of Narrative Art**
Exposition Park, Los Angeles 90007
https://lucasmuseum.org/

**March Field Air Museum**
22550 Van Buren Blvd., Riverside, CA 92518
https://www.marchfield.org/

**Museum of Flying Santa Monica**
3100 Airport Ave., Santa Monica, CA 90405
https://www.museumofflying.org/

**Museum of Latin American Art**
628 Alamitos Avenue, Long Beach, CA 90802
https://molaa.org/

**Natural History Museum**
900 W Exposition Blvd, Los Angeles, CA 90007
https://nhm.org/

**Petersen Automotive Museum**
6060 Wilshire Blvd., Los Angeles, CA 90036
https://petersen.org/

**Pretend City Children's Museum**
29 Hubble, Irvine, CA 92618
https://www.pretendcity.org/

**Ronald Reagan Presidential Library and Museum**
40 Presidential Dr., Simi Valley, CA 93065
https://www.reaganfoundation.org/library-museum/

**Skirball Cultural Center**
2701 N. Sepulveda Blvd., Los Angeles, CA 90049
https://www.skirball.org/

**USC Pacific Asia Museum**
46 North Los Robles Ave., Pasadena 91101
https://pacificasiamuseum.usc.edu/

**Zimmerman Automobile Driving Museum**
610 Lairport St., El Segundo, CA 90245
https://www.automobiledrivingmuseum.org/

## THEME PARKS

**Adventure City**
1238 S Beach Blvd, Anaheim, CA 92804
https://www.adventurecity.com/

**Castle Park**
3500 Polk St., Riverside, CA 92505
https://www.castlepark.com/

**Disneyland and Disney California Adventure**
1313 Harbor Blvd., Anaheim, 92803
https://disneyland.disney.go.com/

**Fiesta Village Family Fun Park**
1405 E Washington St, Colton, CA 92324
https://www.fiestavillage.com/

**Knott's Berry Farm**
8039 Beach Blvd, Buena Park, CA 90620
https://www.knotts.com/

**Great Wolf Lodge**
12681 Harbor Boulevard, Garden Grove CA 92840
https://www.greatwolf.com/southern-california

**Six Flags Magic Mountain**
26101 Magic Mountain Pkwy, Valencia, CA 91355
https://www.sixflags.com/magicmountain

**Universal Studios Hollywood**
100 Universal City Plaza, Universal City, CA 91608
https://www.universalstudioshollywood.com/

**City of Los Angeles Department of Recreation and Parks**
https://www.laparks.org/

**Los Angeles County Parks and Recreation**
https://parks.lacounty.gov/

**Los Angeles County Beaches and Harbors**
Department of Beaches and Harbors
https://beaches.lacounty.gov/

## THINGS TO DO WITH TODDLERS

**Carousel at Santa Monica Pier**
200 Santa Monica Pier, Santa Monica 90401
At the very end of Colorado Blvd and the Pacific Ocean
https://www.santamonicapier.org/

**Beach Time all along the coast**
Los Angeles County Beaches and Harbors
Department of Beaches and Harbors
https://beaches.lacounty.gov/

**Aquarium of the Pacific**
100 Aquarium Way, Long Beach, CA 90802
https://www.aquariumofpacific.org/

**Park Time at one of the many, many parks in SoCal**
City of Los Angeles Department of Recreation and Parks
https://www.laparks.org/

**Los Angeles County Parks and Recreation**
https://parks.lacounty.gov/

**Annenberg Community Beach House**
415 Pacific Coast Highway, Santa Monica, CA 90402
https://www.annenbergbeachhouse.com/

**Discovery Cube Los Angeles and Orange County**
11800 Foothill Blvd, Sylmar, CA 91342
2500 N Main Street, Santa Ana, CA 92805
https://www.discoverycube.org/

**Pretend City Children's Museum**
29 Hubble, Irvine, CA 92618
https://www.pretendcity.org/

**Kidspace Children's Museum**
480 N. Arroyo Blvd., Pasadena, CA 91103
https://kidspacemuseum.org/

**Cayton Children's Museum**
395 Santa Monica Place Mall, Suite 374, Santa Monica 90401
https://www.caytonmuseum.org/

**Petersen Automotive Museum**
6060 Wilshire Blvd., Los Angeles, CA 90036
https://petersen.org/

**Huntington Library, Art Museum and Botanical Gardens**
1151 Oxford Road, San Marino, CA 91108
https://www.huntington.org/

**Descanso Gardens**
1418 Descanso Drive, La Cañada Flintridge, CA 91011
https://www.descansogardens.org/

**Griffith Park Pony Rides**
4400 Crystal Springs Dr., Los Angeles, CA 90027
https://www.griffithparkponyride.com/

**Getty Center Museum**
1200 Getty Center Dr, Los Angeles, CA 90049
https://www.getty.edu/

**Underwood Family Farms**
3370 Sunset Valley Rd., Moorpark, CA 93021
https://www.underwoodfamilyfarms.com/

*Find many more things to do with toddlers on MomsLA.com!*

## AWESOME IDEAS FOR THINGS TO DO WITH TEENS!

**Rock Climbing at an indoor gym**
Sender One (multiple locations)
https://www.senderoneclimbing.com/

**Parasailing, Kayaking, or stand-up Paddleboarding**
Try Marina del Rey
https://www.visitmarinadelrey.com/things-to-do/on-the-water

**Horseback Riding**
Try the Equestrian Center
480 W. Riverside Drive, Burbank 91506
http://thelaec.com/

**Roller Skating at Moonlight Rollerway**
5110 San Fernando Road, Glendale 91204
https://moonlightrollerway.com/

**iFly Indoor Skydiving**
1000 Universal Studios Blvd. #1, Universal City 91608
https://www.iflyworld.com/hollywood/

**Escape Rooms**
Dozens of places to try around SoCal
https://momsla.com/49-great-escape-rooms-in-los-angeles/

**Indoor Kart Racing**
Try K1 Speed (multiple locations)
https://www.k1speed.com/

**Ride the LA River Bike Path**
Miles of trails to explore
https://www.lariver.org/blog/explore-la-river

**Summer Educational Programs**
Learn more about all the options
https://momsla.com/10-incredible-summer-programs-for-los-angeles-high-school-students/

**Six Flags Magic Mountain, Universal Studios Hollywood, Disneyland, Disney California Adventure**
Theme parks will always be a big hit

**Family Hikes**
100s of hiking trails in LA County
https://trails.lacounty.gov/

**Visit Local Colleges**
It's never too soon to start prepping for College!

*Find many more things to do with teens on MomsLA.com!*

# IDEAS FOR SEASONAL FUN
# + ANNUAL EVENTS AND FESTIVALS

## JANUARY
**Tournament of Roses Parade (always held on New Year's Day)**
https://tournamentofroses.com/

**Festival of Human Abilities at Aquarium of the Pacific**
https://www.aquariumofpacific.org/events

**Martin Luther King Day Celebration at CAAM**
https://caamuseum.org/
**And more:** https://momsla.com/celebrating-mlk-day/

**Oshogatsu Family Festival at JANM**
https://www.janm.org/

**Whale Fiesta at Cabrillo Marine Aquarium**
https://www.cabrillomarineaquarium.org/

**Head to the SoCal mountains to play in the snow**
https://momsla.com/best-places-for-snow-play-near-los-angeles/

## FEBRUARY

**African American History Month Festivals at California African American Museum, Aquarium of the Pacific, and other spots**
https://caamuseum.org/
https://www.aquariumofpacific.org/events
**And more:** https://momsla.com/20-ways-celebrate-black-history-month-around-los-angeles/

**Lunar New Year Festivals in Chinatown and other spots**
https://firecracker10k.org/
**And more:** https://momsla.com/where-to-celebrate-lunar-new-year-in-los-angeles/

**Valentine's Day Events at Pretend City and other spots**
https://www.pretendcity.org/
**And more:** https://momsla.com/valentines-day-los-angeles/

## MARCH

**International Children's Festival at Aquarium of the Pacific**
https://www.aquariumofpacific.org/events

**LA Nature Fest at Natural History Museum + opening of the Butterfly Pavilion**
https://nhm.org/

**Grunion Fishtival at Cabrillo Marine Aquarium**
https://www.cabrillomarineaquarium.org/

**LA Marathon**
https://www.lamarathon.com/

**Passover Celebrations (unless Passover occurs in April of that year), at the Skirball** Cultural Center, and other spots
http://www.skirball.org/

**Blessing of the Animals at Olvera Street (Sunday before Easter)**
https://www.olveraevents.com/

**Conejo Valley Days**
https://www.conejovalleydays.us/

## APRIL

**See Spring Wildflowers in Bloom**
https://momsla.com/9-places-see-spring-wildflowers/

**LA Times Festival of Books**
https://events.latimes.com/festivalofbooks/

**Easter Celebrations (unless Easter occurs in March of that year)**
https://momsla.com/fun-ways-celebrate-easter-around-los-angeles/

**California Poppy Festival in Lancaster**
https://www.cityoflancasterca.org/our-city/departments-services/parks-recreation-arts/special-events/california-poppy-festival

**Skirball Puppet Festival**
https://www.skirball.org/

**Santa Clarita Cowboy Festival**
https://cowboyfestival.org/

**Original Renaissance Pleasure Faire**
https://renfair.com/socal/

**Acura Grand Prix of Long Beach**
https://gplb.com/

## MAY

**LA County Fair (new dates beginning in 2022)**
https://www.lacountyfair.com/

**Fiesta Broadway**
https://www.allaccess-la.com/

**Cinco de Mayo Festival Olvera Street**
https://www.olvera-street.com/events

**Fiesta Hermosa**
https://fiestahermosa.net/

**Go Strawberry-Picking**
https://momsla.com/farms-strawberry-picking/

**Great Big Family Play Day**
https://greatbigfamilyplayday.com/

**Celebrate Mother's Day with more than brunch!**
https://momsla.com/mothers-day-brunch-spots-around-los-angeles/

## JUNE

**Celebrate Juneteenth**
https://momsla.com/celebrate-juneteenth/

**Pacific Islander Festival at Aquarium of the Pacific**
https://www.aquariumofpacific.org/

**LA Pride Parade and Festival West Hollywood**
https://lapride.org/

**Pasadena Chalk Festival**
https://www.visitpasadena.com/events/annual-events/chalk-festival/

**Go Cherry-Picking**
https://momsla.com/cherry-picking-farms-los-angeles/

**Leona Valley Cherry Parade and Festival**
https://myleonavalley.org/cherry-parade-%26-festival

**Celebrate Father's Day**
https://momsla.com/fathers-day-los-angeles

**Numerous Outdoor activities take place all Summer long, like concerts and movies**
https://momsla.com/summer/

**Many local Public pools open to keep us cooled off!**
https://momsla.com/12-best-public-pools-around-los-angeles/

## JULY

**4th of July Parades, Block Parties, and Fireworks**
https://momsla.com/best-fourth-of-july-celebrations-in-los-angeles/

**Lotus Festival**
https://www.laparks.org/lotusfestival

**Long Beach Dragon Boat Festival**
https://www.lbdragonboat.com/

**Festival of Arts and Pageant of the Masters in Laguna Beach**
https://www.foapom.com/

**Go Blueberry Picking**
https://momsla.com/pick-blueberries-los-angeles/

**Cool off at a Water Park**
https://momsla.com/best-water-parks-around-los-angeles/

## AUGUST
**Fiesta La Ballona (unless schedule has changed to Fall)**
https://www.fiestalaballona.org/Home

**LA Taco Festival**
http://www.latacofestival.com/

**Nisei Week Japanese Festival Little Tokyo**
https://niseiweek.org/festival/

**Go Camping**
https://momsla.com/best-family-campgrounds-around-los-angeles/

**CicLAvia - open streets event takes place 3-4 times per year in different parts of Los Angeles)**
https://www.ciclavia.org/

## SEPTEMBER
**Dino Fest at Natural History Museum + Spider Pavilion opens**
https://nhm.org/

**Fiesta Hermosa 2nd time**
https://fiestahermosa.net/

**Moopetam Native American Festival at Aquarium of the Pacific**
https://www.aquariumofpacific.org/

**Abbot Kinney Festival**
https://www.abbotkinney.org/

**Annual Watts Tower Day of the Drum and Jazz Festival**
https://www.wattstowers.org/

## OCTOBER

**Numerous Halloween Events all over SoCal**
https://momsla.com/things-to-do-with-kids-in-los-angeles-to-celebrate-halloween/

**Many Harvest Festivals in SoCal**
https://momsla.com/harvest-festivals-los-angeles/

**Visit Underwood Family Farms**
https://www.underwoodfamilyfarms.com/

**Mr. Bones Pumpkin Patch**
https://mrbonespumpkinpatch.com/

**Nights of the Jack**
https://nightsofthejack.com/

**Carved at Descanso Gardens**
https://www.descansogardens.org/

**Go Apple-Picking**
https://momsla.com/go-apple-picking/

## NOVEMBER

**Numerous Dia de Los Muertos Celebrations**
https://momsla.com/celebrate-dia-de-los-muertos-around-los-angeles/

**Hollywood Forever Cemetery**
https://hollywoodforever.com/culture/

**Forest Lawn Cemetery**
https://forestlawn.com/events/

**Olvera Street**
https://www.olvera-street.com/events

**Autumn Festival at Aquarium of the Pacific**
https://www.aquariumofpacific.org/

**Volunteer to Help Serve Thanksgiving Dinner to Those in Need**
https://losangelesmission.org/

**Hollywood Christmas Parade (Sunday after Thanksgiving)**
https://thehollywoodchristmasparade.org/

## DECEMBER

**Numerous Hanukkah Festivals and Events (unless Hanukkah occurs in November that year)**
https://momsla.com/20-hanukkah-celebrations-around-los-angeles/

**Numerous Christmas Festivals and Events**
https://momsla.com/best-christmas-holiday-events-los-angeles/

**Hanukkah at the Skirball**
https://www.skirball.org/

**Enchanted Forest of Light at Descanso Gardens**
https://www.descansogardens.org/

**Candy Cane Lane neighborhood events, like El Segundo and Altadena**
https://momsla.com/where-to-see-holiday-lights-in-los-angeles/

**Christmas on the Farm at Underwood Family Farms**
https://www.underwoodfamilyfarms.com/

**Mission Inn Museum Riverside Festival of Lights**
https://www.missioninn.com/about/festival-of-lights

**LA County Holiday Celebration at Dorothy Chandler/Music Center**
https://www.musiccenter.org/tickets-free-events/tmc-arts/l-a-county-holiday-celebration/

**See a Holiday Boat Parade**
https://momsla.com/christmas-boat-parades-southern-california/

**Celebrate Las Posadas Olvera Street**
https://www.olvera-street.com/events

**Celebrate New Year's Eve**
https://momsla.com/best-family-friendly-new-years-events-in-southern-california/

**Head back to the mountains for snow play**
https://momsla.com/best-places-for-snow-play-near-los-angeles/


*Find more information about all these annual festivals and events—and so much more—on MomsLA.com!*

# INDEX

www.ingramcontent.com/pod-product-compliance
Lightning Source LLC
Chambersburg PA
CBHW070714130626
46553CB00005B/1992